STORYTELLING

EILEEN COLWELL

Storytelling

The Thimble Press
in association with
Westminster College, Oxford

In memory of U.C., who loved to
listen to my stories and whose
professional knowledge helped
me in the telling of them.

Storytelling comes from The Thimble Press,
publishers since 1970 of *Signal*, the thrice-yearly
journal devoted to books and reading for
children and young people, and the Signal Bookguides.

Westminster College, Oxford, collaborates with
The Thimble Press to promote the education of children
through literature. The College offers
a full range of courses for teachers in partnership
with the profession. Further information from
Westminster College, North Hinksey, Oxford OX2 9AT.

ISBN 0 903355 35 3

Keyed at The Thimble Press
Lockwood, Station Road, South Woodchester,
Stroud, Glos. GL5 5EQ
Typesetting by Avonset, Midsomer Norton, Bath
Printed in Great Britain by
Short Run Press, Exeter

CONTENTS

Acknowledgement & Illustrations List, 6

Preface, 7

1. Storytelling Then and Now, 9

2. The Storyteller, 16

3. What Shall I Tell?, 19
Stories for Preschool Children

4. What Shall I Tell?, 30
Stories for Five- to Twelve-year-olds

5. Adapting the Story for Telling, 44

6. Remembering the Story, 53

7. Improving Your Voice and Speech, 66

8. Facing the Audience, 70

9. Special Situations, 79

10. Storytelling Here and There, 85

100 + Storytelling Sources, 92

ACKNOWLEDGEMENT

The stories and books I write about in the following pages are those that appeal especially to me and that are most appropriate to the way I tell stories. Every storyteller will have his or her own favourites, of course, and I am grateful to Mary Steele and Beverley Mathias for the suggestions they have made in the booklists on pages 92 to 96 and for other helpful comments. Mary Steele has also found currently available sources for many of the stories included in the main text, and these are indicated in the listings at the end of each chapter.

ILLUSTRATIONS LIST

Page 14. Wood engraving by Hannah Firmin for *Folk-tales of the British Isles* by Kevin Crossley-Holland (Faber)

Page 20. One of Raymond Briggs's line drawings for Wanda Gág's 'Gone is Gone' in *The Fairy Tale Treasury* by Virginia Haviland (Hamish Hamilton)

Page 23. Illustration by Jill Bennett for E.M. Almedingen's 'Volkh's Journey to the East' in *Imagine That!* by Sara & Stephen Corrin (Faber)

Page 33. Illustration by Joseph Olubo for 'Anancy and the Making of the Bro Title' in *Anancy-Spiderman* by James Berry (Walker)

Page 37. Chapter head by Ann Strugnell for 'The Indian Cinderella' in *The Faber Book of North American Legends* by Virginia Haviland (Faber)

Page 42. Illustration by Alan Howard for 'The Burning of Berg-thorsknoll' from *Njal's Saga* in *Northern Lights: Legends, Sagas and Folk-tales* by Kevin Crossley-Holland (Faber)

Page 54. Illustration by Judith Bledsoe for 'The Tale of a Turnip' in *Tell Me a Story* by Eileen Colwell (Young Puffin)

Page 75. Illustration by Jerry Pinkney for 'Brer Rabbit Gets Even' in *The Tales of Uncle Remus: The Adventures of Brer Rabbit* by Julius Lester (Bodley Head)

PREFACE

The love of stories is universal. For generations, parents have heard the insistent cry: 'Tell me a story!' And, given the opportunity, adults love stories as much as children. It is no accident that the greater proportion of books borrowed from libraries – by both children and adults – are stories of one sort or another, and that hosts of people watch television simply to find out 'what happens next'.

For over fifty years I have told stories to thousands of children of all ages and from many nations. I have seen four hundred nuns in a gloomy London hall rocking with laughter at a funny story, and a group of refugee women from Central Europe smiling through tears at a story they had heard as children in their own country. I have talked to adults about storytelling in all kinds of centres and colleges, and have been a guest storyteller in the United States, Canada, Japan and European countries where English is understood. Students and teachers, children and parents, all are united by the experience of listening to a story together. You have only to watch one child – or fifty – listening to a well-told tale to realize how much pleasure stories can give.

This is a very personal book. I originally wrote it more than ten years ago, basing it on my own experience and intending it as a guide and encouragement to would-be storytellers everywhere – librarians, teachers, playgroup leaders, parents. For this new edition the text has been substantially revised, the beginning of the book recast, and additions made to the booklists.

Thanks are due to many librarian friends, particularly Hertfordshire County libraries, who have shared their experience of storytelling with me. A special thank-you to the many, many children and adults who, over the years, have shared my stories and made the telling of them such a happy experience.

1

Storytelling
Then and Now

The storyteller of today is a link in the long chain of story-tellers stretching back into the past and ahead into the future. She is practising a traditional art in which the emphasis is entirely on the spoken word – unlike other contemporary arts that rely on visual image. Before the days of writing, when the spoken word was the only means of communication, stories were an essential and enjoyable part of life. Without written records, the history and laws of a tribe had to be remembered and passed on orally, often in the form of stories. Through stories, patterns of behaviour and moral truths can be conveyed in ways easy to understand and remember. The give-and-take between storyteller and audience has always been a vital educational experience and provides a stimulus for speech and self-expression. From the beginning, storytelling has had value and significance for everyone in the community.

Two of the most common types of stories were very likely what Arthur Ransome called the 'Warning Example' and the 'Embroidered Exploit'. Mothers of every generation have known the necessity and effectiveness of cautioning children against danger by an example in story form. 'Once there was a child,' says the mother, 'who *would* go down to the river although his mother told him not to. Listen to what happened to him . . .' Such warning stories would often be aimed not only at children but at any member of the community who offended against the laws of the tribe. The 'Embroidered

Exploit' would have originated as the factual report of a hunter's encounter with some wild animal, for example. Exaggeration was inevitable with each retelling, so that in course of time the exploit assumed such magnitude that it was far beyond the capabilities of any human being. Thus an everyday event grew into an extraordinary feat performed by a hero.

Stories also developed as a means of explaining natural phenomena, such as thunder and lightning, earthquake and flood, and the changing seasons. Inevitably such tales required supernatural beings: in Norse mythology Thor beat out thunder with his hammer, and in the Greek myths Ceres' distress over the rape of her daughter Persephone could cause drought and disrupt the seasons. People's ignorance of natural processes resulted in a wealth of imaginative stories.

J.R.R. Tolkien likens 'Story' to a pot of soup into which almost everything has been dropped – scraps of history, religion, legends, dreams, magic and magical objects – and out of which almost anything can come. It is certain, however, that stories have always been travellers, carried by Roman legionaries, pilgrims, crusaders, sailors, gypsies, and exchanged with others from many lands. In all centuries, not least our own, refugees fleeing from invading armies have been able to forget their loneliness for a time as they told the stories of their homeland.

In the beginning everyone was a storyteller, but inevitably one member of the tribe would excel in skill and effectiveness. As time went on, such people would devote their whole lives to remembering and telling the tribal stories of past history and heroic deeds. These early professional storytellers established a custom that was to endure in many forms and in many lands. They usually sang or chanted their stories, perhaps in simple verse forms to the music of a primitive, harp-like instrument, and they had many names. In northern lands, in what is now Scandinavia, a storyteller was known as a *skald*. Skalds rode with the king into battle so that they could sing of his valour, and they occupied a privileged position in his retinue: they could expect to receive a harp from the king and a ring from the queen and to be ransomed if captured in war. In Wales the storyteller was called *bard*; to become a master bard an apprentice had to learn a great number of stories, which had come down through the generations by word of mouth. In Ireland the term for storyteller was *ollamh* or *seanachie*, and each of them could recite two hundred tales. One eighth-century storyteller told a different tale each night from Samain to Beltane (1 November to 1 May)!

There have been storytellers in England for many centuries. In the fourth century the gleeman Widsith sang and spoke a story in the mead hall and was given a collar of beaten gold and a ring in return. Bede relied considerably on 'the traditions of our forefathers' – stories and poems passed on orally – in his *Ecclesiastical History of the English People*. Caedmon of Whitby composed not only sacred poems but secular rhymes for gleemen to sing.

With the coming of the Normans the Saxon gleemen almost disappeared. They could not compete with the more sophisticated Norman minstrels, especially as the language of the court was now French. These minstrels were welcome everywhere, for they were often the only means of entertainment in the long winter evenings. Storytelling was an accepted part of daily life, and in the draughty baronial halls of castles the lord, his family, servants and men-at-arms would gather round the fire to listen to tales told by some traveller or minstrel. Whether in manor house or peasant dwelling, someone would tell a story to keep the darkness and its perils away. It was only common courtesy to repay hospitality with a story. 'England was conquered to the music of verse and settled to the sound of the harp,' says the historian Stopford Brooke.

The minstrel was a distinctive figure. Dressed in unusual, brightly coloured clothes, his instrument in hand, he wandered about the country, visiting castle, manor house or market place, reciting the old tales, sometimes in verse, sometimes in prose, of Bevis of Southampton, Beowulf, Guy of Warwick, and many more. Sometimes he had a retinue which included a buffoon to make people laugh, a tumbler (juggler) and a musician. Minstrels were present at every important occasion, and had a great deal of influence, for they could win the ear of the people and weave complaints against unpopular taxes or public figures into the stories and song. Edward I, for example, had many minstrels in his train, including two women, Matill Makejoye and Pearl in the Egg.

Storytelling was by no means confined to these specialists but was a familiar feature of everyday life until the fifteenth century. As we know from *The Canterbury Tales*, on every pilgrimage travellers told stories to while away the tedium of the journey. Everywhere, sermons were illustrated by stories until the religious reformer Wycliffe and other churchmen denounced the custom on the grounds that such tales kept pagan beliefs alive.

The invention of printing in the fifteenth century gradually brought to an end the telling of tales by professional minstrels whose public was mainly the richer members of the community. With the foundation of schools and the spread of education, many people in the upper and merchant classes learned to read for themselves. For the less well-off, ballad singers who recited or sang popular verses about topical events or the deeds of folk heroes took the place of minstrels. But the same stories survived in various forms. Among the first of Caxton's printed works were *Reynard the Fox* and Malory's *Morte d'Arthur*, which was based on old French and Celtic tales of romance kept alive by minstrels for generations.

Even with the advent of printing the storytelling tradition lingered among the ordinary people in town and country. Stories were passed on, usually by older men and women to their families or to small gatherings of neighbours. In *The Anatomy of Melancholy*, written in the sixteenth century, Robert Burton claims that the customary recreations of people in winter were 'merry tales of errant knights, queens, lovers, lords, ladies, giants, dwarfs, thieves, cheaters, witches, fayries, goblins . . . which some delight to hear, some to tell, and all are well pleased with'. The traditional material transmitted orally consisted largely of fairy and folk tales, romances and hero stories.

By degrees the custom of telling tales as part of everyday life disappeared. Why was this? One theory holds that storytelling declined because the rhythm of life changed with the Industrial Revolution. No longer did men and women carry on their traditional working skills at home in the evenings while someone told a story. Now the men, and often the women and children, worked in factories for long hours. The weariness of the people and the sheer lack of time were not conducive to the telling of tales. The invention of better lighting for the home had altered the old pattern of the day. Newspapers and books took over from the storyteller's memory. The oral tradition was dying out, and by the nineteenth century learned men were collecting the old stories as folklore rather than as living material to be shared and enjoyed.

Although storytelling was no longer a daily occasion in nineteenth-century town life, it still lingered in remote parts of the countryside. These rural storytellers could recite many tales of heroic quests, exploits and legendary history. A collector of folk tales recorded no less than 375 tales from Peig Sayers, a teller of Gaelic tales who lived all her life on the bleak Great Basket Island off the coast of Kerry. She was known as 'the queen of Gaelic storytellers' and died as recently as 1958. In the introduction to her book, *An Old Woman's Reflections*, she describes a typical storytelling:

> In a whitewashed kitchen in the glen the peat-fire glows like a berry, and the cricket – 'the cock of the ashes' – sings. And the tangle of Gaelic voices singles out as the Storyteller spreads his fingers for attention and begins his tale.

In the 1970s an old Irishman told me that his most vivid childhood memory was of listening to an Irish seanachie, a Gaelic teller of legendary romances, telling stories in a cottage within the sound of the sea.

Storytelling is still a living tradition in many countries where education and books are not readily and widely available. In Morocco storytellers are found in market

places, and in Egypt Bedouins listen to professional storytellers with loud clapping of hands. In Java the honoured
dalang chants tales from the Ramayana, moving puppets
against a screen. And in Nigeria villagers welcome travelling
storytellers whose tales play an important part in educating
children in tribal customs and tradition. Sometimes what is
sacred or precious is given a reverence by the human voice
that cannot be conveyed on the printed page.

In the western world the art of storytelling is being con-
sciously revived after years of decline. In Britain, Canada,
Australia and the United States regular storytelling workshops are held for teachers, librarians and students. They
listen to stories and are taught how to tell them. Festivals are
held, courses are offered. A brief account of this revival is
included in Chapter Ten.

Britain has had many storytellers whose names may only
have been known locally but who kept the art alive and
shared stories with children. In 1922 an English teacher,
Marie Shedlock, travelled through war-torn France telling
stories to the children of devastated areas in their own
language. She was a wonderful interpreter of Andersen's
stories and practised her art in both America and England.
Better known here was the name of Elizabeth Clark, an
inspired storyteller who gave demonstrations to colleges of
education, libraries and universities. I still come across

14

teachers who remember the way this unassuming woman could entrance large gatherings of students. Elizabeth Clark's collections of stories retold from folk tales, legends and literature are still excellent material. All her stories were tested with children before being included in her books.

Whatever the origin of stories, the same basic patterns appear again and again round the world, passing from mouth to mouth and from generation to generation for centuries and giving pleasure to countless hearers. For example, 'Nix Nought Nothing', one of those stories in which a father, unaware of his son's birth, promises to give 'nix nought nothing' to an enemy in order to save his own life, is found in India, Egypt, Greece, North and South America, Samoa, Russia and Africa. 'Puss-in-Boots' originated in Arabia, travelled to Italy and France, then to Scandinavia, Africa, the East, and Russia. Joseph Jacobs once noted that he had edited an English version of an Italian adaptation of a Spanish translation of a Latin version of a Hebrew translation of an Arabic translation of an Indian original. Names and background may alter, but basic plots remain. And behind all these ancient tales, and before all written literature, is the voice of the anonymous storyteller.

BOOKS & STORIES MENTIONED

'Nix Nought Nothing', in Joseph Jacobs's *English Fairy Tales*, Dover

'Puss in Books', in *Sleeping Beauty and Other Favourite Fairy Tales* trans. Angela Carter, Gollancz

Peig Sayers, *An Old Woman's Reflections*, Oxford University Press

2

The Storyteller

Why *tell* a story? Why not read it? Both ways of communicating stories have a place, but there is an enormous difference between the two, for the adult involved and the child listening. The reader must always be conscious of the printed page before her and can only occasionally look at the audience, while the teller is free to speak directly to the listeners and to watch their reactions. For children the voice and personality of the storyteller add richness and vitality to the story. The occasion takes on an immediacy and becomes a personal experience for teller and audience alike, and an intimate relationship is established between the two.

Storytelling has three essential elements:

– the story
– the storyteller
– the audience.

Storytelling cannot be a success unless there is harmony between these three.

First, the story: a narrative of real or fictitious happenings, usually short enough to be told in one session. The variety of stories available to the modern storyteller is infinite: stories of everyday life, the world of nature, the supernatural, magic and fantastic. They inspire laughter and tears, bring home the virtues of courage, kindness and loyalty, compassion and wonder; portray the ever-present struggle between good and evil; touch the depths of human and spiritual experience. This great variety means that anyone who wants to be a storyteller can be sure to find stories that are just right for her.

The link between story and audience is the storyteller. There is no infallible recipe for the making of a storyteller; the potential is in everyone. Even the least eloquent of beings can give a convincing account of his or her own personal experiences. This is simply because your own experiences are of absorbing interest to you, so you feel deeply about them and want to talk about them with others. It is easy to describe what has happened to you because you remember it in detail and can *see* it as you put it into words.

The essential ingredients of successful storytelling are:

- interest in what you are describing and involvement in the story;
- a detailed visual picture of the story's events;
- a desire that the listener should understand and share your feelings.

Some rare individuals are natural storytellers and are able to tell stories with ease and confidence. Most people, however, are unsure of their ability while others are even convinced that storytelling is totally beyond them. This is a fallacy, for anyone who is willing to spend some time in study and practice can become a good storyteller. As in life, you can only learn by trial and error, and encouragement is vital if you are to gain confidence.

Certain qualities, however, are an advantage for the would-be storyteller. A creative imagination can give life and colour to a story; a feeling for drama and a degree of skill in portraying character will lend the life and excitement that children so much enjoy. A capacity for seeing the funny side of life on difficult occasions, the humility to laugh at your own affectations, a readiness to share children's rather slap-stick sense of humour, all help enormously. Similarly, a storyteller should have the grace to acknowledge a wrong choice of story, insufficient preparation, dullness in presentation: these are the storyteller's fault, and cannot be blamed on some strange lack of sensitivity in the audience. A wide knowledge of books of all kinds is invaluable, and its corollary, a good vocabulary, ensures command of the most effective words and a liveliness in telling. Above all, you must believe in the value of telling stories to children, or the necessary preparation will be without heart or purpose.

Here, I am referring mainly to storytelling based on published material, some of which may be original and some based on oral sources. To today's multicultural society people from India, Africa and the Caribbean bring different conventions of oral storytelling. There are schools where parents and elders of the local community are invited to tell stories in their mother tongue – sometimes adapting traditional tales to reflect their current life, sometimes telling stories in exactly the way they have been told for generations. Often these will be dual-language storytelling sessions so that everyone can understand.

Whatever the style of storytelling, children's response is shown by complete absorption, a feeling of anticipation or sadness according to the mood of the story. These responses are tangible, but there are others which we may never know about. The storyteller may think the story will soon be forgotten, but for a child it may become a treasured memory for years to come. I have told stories long enough to have had the experience of hearing an adult, once a child in one of my storytelling sessions, say, 'Do you remember that story you used to tell us? I have never forgotten it. Now I am sharing it with my own children.'

3

What Shall I Tell?

Stories for Preschool Children

The hardest part of storytelling is selecting a story, not because there is a shortage of material but because there is so much to choose from. Yet selection is also a most interesting and rewarding exercise. In looking for a story to tell, you will extend your knowledge and appreciation of all kinds of literature, discovering new and challenging byways, learning discrimination as you select.

Choosing a story is always a very personal matter, for unless it appeals to you, it will be difficult to tell with enthusiasm and conviction. I have seen would-be storytellers using stories which are suitable in theory but which they do not enjoy themselves. The result was inevitably disastrous. If you really like a story and are eager to share it, you will be halfway to success. Without this qualification, the audience is likely to be apathetic or restless simply because you cannot tell it with conviction.

An important point to remember when selecting stories is that what may appeal to the eye may not appeal to the ear. Some stories are for reading, some for telling. The structure of the story as a whole, the length of the sentences, the general pattern, are different in the two kinds of story. Consider, for instance, the differences between Andersen's 'The Little Mermaid' and Wanda Gág's *Gone is Gone*, a version of the folk tale about the man who thought he could keep house better than his wife. Andersen's story opens with a long description of the world under the sea where the mermaids live, and it is several pages later before the Little Mermaid attains her desire to see 'the upper world', which is the beginning of the story. In *Gone is Gone* the story begins at once with a minimum of description:

> This man, his name was Fritzl – his wife, her name was Liesi. They had a little baby, Kinndli by name, and Spitz who was a dog.

The Little Mermaid's story is told in long sentences and paragraphs, using a wide vocabulary and poetic images. In Wanda Gág's story, sentences are short, the vocabulary familiar and domestic and the plot uncomplicated, so that the story is easy to comprehend at the first hearing. The emphasis in Andersen is on feeling so that the story moves slowly and needs to be read thoughtfully as an imaginative and emotional experience. *Gone is Gone* moves quickly from one amusing incident to the next until the expected climax when Liesi comes home to find chaos. The title phrase, repeated many times, invites children to join in, and there is a feeling of spontaneity, the mark of a story that has been recounted by many tellers. It is obvious that here is a story to be *told* – and equally obvious that 'The Little Mermaid' needs to be read to oneself so that its beauty, pathos and underlying meaning may be fully appreciated and lingered over.

With experience the storyteller learns to distinguish almost instinctively between a story for telling and a story for reading. The beginner should look out for these characteristics:

> – direct colloquial speech that establishes a relationship between teller and audience;
> – a minimum of description;
> – plenty of action.

The way a story is written can add beauty and life to what might otherwise seem rather ordinary material. An author's individual handling of words, the manner of expressing emotion, of giving life to a character, of evoking a landscape – all these have a part in building an author's style. Take the old fairy tale 'The Sleeping Beauty' in Arthur Rackham's *Fairy Book*. The princess has just pricked her finger on the spindle:

> . . . Though it was but a small wound, she immediately fainted and fell to the floor . . . There she lay, as beautiful as an angel, with the colour still lingering in her lips and cheeks, but her eyes were tightly closed . . .

Here is Walter de la Mare's description of the same incident in *Tales Told Again*:

> Before even the blood had welled up to the size of a bead upon her thumb, the wicked magic of the Fairy Woman began to enter into her body. Slowly, drowsily, the Princess's eyelids began to descend over her dark blue eyes; her two hands slid softly down on either side of her; her head drooped lower and lower towards her pillow. She put out her two hands, as if groping her way; sighed; sank lower; and soon she had fallen fast, fast asleep.

Note how evocative and musical this passage is – and almost soporific in its effect! The stories a child hears can enrich the vocabulary and train the ear to respond to the music and rhythm of words. And children can certainly appreciate these qualities. A nine-year-old wrote this about words:

The boring words –
I look at them dragging their feet.
But when the exciting marvellous words
Jump out, I dance and sing with them.
The boring, dreary words
Slip back into the book.
Good luck to them!
I like the words
Which liven me up.

Every story needs time and energy to prepare, so it is never worth choosing one you feel is trivial or commonplace. Such stories can only give momentary pleasure rather than a lasting experience. The vulgar, the cynical, the sadistic, have no place in stories for children, widespread though they are in everyday life. The emphasis, I believe, must be on qualities worth emulating: loyalty, courage and kindness.

The audience must be taken into account when choosing a story to tell. It may be only boys or only girls, or both; it may be children from homes where books are part of everyday life or children who never hear stories or see books, or both. The age of children in the audience will influence your choice, which is largely a matter of common sense. Normally if you tell a fairy story to boys of thirteen or read *Hamlet* to a group of infants, as I once heard an eminent actor do, you must accept the consequences!

Problems arise when the storyteller is faced, perhaps unexpectedly, with a group of mixed age range, say six- to ten-year-olds. Shall we choose a story for the older children or the younger? I have found that some stories can be enjoyed by a wide age range, particularly folk tales. 'The Magic Umbrella' by Rose Fyleman, the Japanese tale of 'The Magic Kettle' by Rhoda Power, 'Two of Everything' by Alice Ritchie, are successful with a varied age group. All are funny and can be told simply so that younger children can

understand them. The Russian adventure tale 'Volkh's Journey to the East' by E.M. Almedingen has great attraction, for each child can keep count of the number of wishes the young hero has left, and the suspense of the situation holds the attention of all ages. I have also found, on numerous occasions, that an appeal to the older members of the group to wait patiently while I tell a story to the younger ones is successful. They are then free to enjoy a younger story without embarrassment while at the same time feeling virtuous and kindly. Whatever the age, each child takes from the story what he or she is *ready* to appeciate.

It is important to treat children as sensible beings and as equals. Even a hint of condescension not only causes resentment but is unfair to children and creates a gap between them and the adult. Whatever the age group, it is wise to choose a story that will stretch the listener. Most children look forward with touching optimism to the day when they will be grown-up, and no child likes to be treated as being incapable of understanding a story that seems to be

a little beyond him. In fact, most children understand much more when listening to a story than when reading it for themselves.

Sometimes storytelling is an impromptu affair for the storyteller, snatched from a busy period because a small group of restless children offers an opportunity for the introduction of a story. For such occasions no plan can be made in advance other than ensuring that you have a good stock of stories to draw upon. For the more formal occasions in library or school, some kind of programme is prudent if the best use is to be made of the time available. In schools there is usually a set time for stories and the age group is constant so selection is easier. In libraries stories usually must be told at a regular time to fit into the schedule of opening hours and staff duties. Attendance is voluntary, and audiences cannot always be divided into age groups, so they are likely to be of mixed ages. The storyteller may recognize some of the children, but by no means all. It is harder therefore to plan a programme in advance but advisable to do so all the same.

For preschool children in playgroups, nursery schools or libraries a storytelling programme should not last more than half an hour. The attention span of three- to five-year-olds is short, and they are too full of energy to sit still and listen for a longer period. In fact, even a thirty-minute session should be broken up with a more active interlude.

In playgroups it is often difficult to persuade children to leave their activities and games to hear a story. Storytime must prove itself a pleasurable part of the day with something interesting and exciting to offer. Once established, this quieter period can become something children look forward to. The opportunity storytime provides to *look* and *listen* is invaluable to a child's development at this early stage.

The main source of stories for young children are picture books and collections of simple tales like those found in the Young Puffin series. Children love stories of pets, home life, shopping with mother, walks in the park – the everyday life they know. Stories in which machines, cars and planes have human characteristics – Diana Ross's *The Little Red Engine*, for instance, or Val Biro's *Gumdrop* – are usually particular favourites.

I have found it advisable to break up the storytime for young children into three parts: a picture book, an interval of participation, and a second story, with a concluding rhyme to round things off.

First, the picture book. Physically the book should be large enough for all the group to see – fifteen or twenty children at one time is the limit. Pictures should be bold, clear and brightly coloured. Hold the book facing the children at a suitable height and turn the pages slowly as you tell the story, allowing time for your audience to absorb each picture and relate it to the words.

The text of a picture book to be shared in such a way must be simple and direct:

> Sophie opened the door, and there was a big, furry, stripy tiger. The tiger said, 'Excuse me, but I'm very hungry. Do you think I could have tea with you?' Sophie's mummy said, 'Of course, come in.' (from Judith Kerr's *The Tiger Who Came to Tea*)

Repetition in words or pictures is essential. Pat Hutchins's *Rosie's Walk* is a brilliant example, with its repetitive pictures showing Rosie the hen strutting across page after page, supremely unconscious of her danger from the pursuing fox. In *The Elephant and the Bad Baby* by Elfrida Vipont and Raymond Briggs, both elephant and baby go 'rumpeta, rumpeta, all down the road', a phrase repeated time after time to the pleasurable anticipation of children. The sound of words can seem very funny to them, and invented words of the 'ploshy-sploshy' type can usually be relied upon to excite chuckles.

However simple the story, something must happen in the text and pictures. Beautiful abstract paintings and drawings can never have the universal appeal of a good story told in pictures and words, I believe, and illustrations must always be representational enough for the child to recognize.

Perennial favourites are the 'Babar' stories, the 'Mr Gumpy' books, and *Harry the Dirty Dog*.

After the picture-book story, it is time for a change to something a little more active that will involve the children. This is when finger plays – rhymes accompanied by movements of the fingers and hands – are useful, not only because they demand participation but because they help children to co-ordinate hand movements. Watch a young child and you will realize how difficult this can be!

Take a very simple example of a finger play:

'A little mouse hid in a hole'
[place the first finger of the left hand between thumb and finger of the closed fist of the right hand]
'Hid softly in a little hole. When all was quiet as quiet could be'
[at this point every child is still, eyes fixed on the teller's hands; pause for a second or two, then withdraw the left-hand finger quickly]
'OUT POPPED HE!'

'I was first!' cries a child. 'I was firster!' shouts another. After a few repetitions, every child is joining in.

Finger plays are simple games that involve children both physically and mentally. Collections of such rhymes to use from babyhood onwards are to be found in Norah Montgomerie's *This Little Pig Went to Market* and Elizabeth Matterson's *This Little Puffin*. . . The latter includes action songs and musical games for more active occasions. The words of these rhymes suggest the actions, and the storyteller can easily invent new variations.

Nursery rhymes are also good material for the preschool storytime interval. Today these rhymes are often neglected, and many children learn only two or three because this is all their parents readily remember. Nursery rhymes are important, for they are the child's first introduction to a simple form of poetry, rhyme and rhythm. They have survived – some of them for centuries – because their form and the pictures they evoke make them easy to memorize. 'Little Boy

Blue', 'Baa baa, black sheep', and the charming 'I had a little nut tree' are good examples.

At this stage children learn quickly through repetition and enjoy chanting or singing nursery rhymes. If actions can be fitted to words, so much the better, as this makes them still easier to remember. 'Sing a song of sixpence' is a favourite for this reason. It has many actable lines: 'The Queen was in the parlour/ Eating bread and honey/ . . . down came a blackbird/ And pecked off her nose.' (Some children need reassurance about this!) Useful collections of nursery rhymes are Nicola Bayley's, illustrated with beautiful, detailed full-colour paintings, and Iona and Peter Opie's *Puffin Book of Nursery Rhymes*.

Occasionally the interval can be more active, with the children marching round the room to the tune of 'The Grand Old Duke of York' or playing some simple game like 'Here we come gathering nuts and may'. But this takes up time, and it can be difficult to recapture the children's attention afterwards. It is best to save such activities for special occasions, to create a party atmosphere at Christmas or before the summer break.

After the interval the children will be ready to listen to the second and final story. This need not have pictures, provided it is uncomplicated, brief, and concerned with familar things children can visualize for themselves. The well-loved traditional tale 'The Three Bears' is a good example, and there are many collections of other suitable stories. For instance, *Playtime Stories* by Joyce Donoghue, tales of young children at home; my own collections, *Tell Me a Story* and its successors; the 'Ponder and William' stories by Barbara Softly; the 'Milly-Molly-Mandy' stories by Joyce L. Brisley, old-fashioned perhaps, but still enjoyed by children for their homeliness. Children love to laugh, so look out for funny stories like *Mrs Pepperpot* or Donald Bisset's 'The Quacking Pillarbox'.

Here is an example of a preschool storytelling programme, following the pattern of picture-book story, an interval of finger plays, and a second story. A closing rhyme or simple ritual can conclude the programme.

Preschool Storytime

[Lively tune on tape recorder as children come in. Don't forget to ask if any child has a birthday.]

PICTURE BOOKS — *Wild Animals*   Brian Wildsmith
The Very Hungry Caterpillar   Eric Carle

INTERVAL
Finger plays — 'A little Mouse hid in a hole . . .'
'Here is a tree with leaves so green'
'Five currant buns in a baker's shop'
(From *This Little Puffin* . . .)

Nursery rhymes — 'Baa, baa, black sheep'
(learnt the previous week)
'Ride a cock-horse . . .'

STORY WITHOUT PICTURES — 'The Dog that Had No Name'
Leila Berg (from *Time for a Story*
Eileen Colwell)

CLOSING RHYME — 'Two little hands go clap, clap, clap.
Two little feet go tap, tap, tap.
Two little arms high in the air,
ONE BIG JUMP UP FROM
THE CHAIR!'

BOOKS & STORIES MENTIONED

E.M. Almedingen, 'Volkh's Journey to the East', in *Imagine That!* ed. Sara & Stephen Corrin, Faber / Puffin

Hans C. Andersen, 'The Little Mermaid', in Erik Haugaard's *Hans Andersen – His Classic Fairy Tales*, Gollancz

Nicola Bayley, *Nicola Bayley's Book of Nursery Rhymes*, Cape / Picture Puffin

Leila Berg, 'The Dog That Had No Name', in *Time for a Story* ed. Eileen Colwell, Young Puffin

Val Biro, *Gumdrop, The Adventures of a Vintage Car*, Hodder & Stoughton / Picture Puffin

Donald Bisset, 'The Quacking Pillarbox', in *Time for a Story* ed. Eileen Colwell, Young Puffin

Joyce L. Brisley, *Milly-Molly-Mandy Stories* and *Milly-Molly-Mandy Again,* both Young Puffin

Jean de Brunhoff, *The Story of Babar the Little Elephant*, Methuen / Magnet

John Burningham, *Mr Gumpy's Outing*, Cape / Picture Puffin

John Burningham, *Mr Gumpy's Motor Car*, Cape / Picture Puffin

Eric Carle, *The Very Hungry Caterpillar*, Hamish Hamilton / Puffin

Eileen Colwell, *Tell Me a Story*, Young Puffin

Eileen Colwell, *The Youngest Storybook*, Bodley Head, o.p.

Walter de la Mare, 'Sleeping Beauty', in *Tales Told Again*, Faber, o.p.

Joyce Donoghue, *Playtime Stories*, Young Puffin

Rose Fyleman, 'The Magic Umbrella', in *More Stories for Under-Fives* ed. Sara & Stephen Corrin, Young Puffin

Wanda Gág, *Gone is Gone*, in Virginia Haviland's *Fairy Tale Treasury*, Hamish Hamilton / Picture Puffin

Margaret B. Graham & Gene Zion, *Harry the Dirty Dog*, Bodley Head / Picture Puffin

Pat Hutchins, *Rosie's Walk*, Bodley Head / Puffin

Judith Kerr, *The Tiger Who Came to Tea*, Collins / Picture Lion

Norah Montgomerie, *This Little Pig Went to Market*, Bodley Head, o.p.

Elizabeth Matterson, *This Little Puffin . . .* , Young Puffin

Iona & Peter Opie, *The Puffin Book of Nursery Rhymes*, Young Puffin

Rhoda Power, 'The Magic Kettle', in *Stories from Everywhere*, Dobson, o.p.

Alf Prøysen, *Little Old Mrs Pepperpot*, Hutchinson / Beaver

Arthur Rackham, 'The Sleeping Beauty', in *Fairy Book*, Harrap, o.p.

Alice Ritchie, 'Two of Everything', in *More Stories for Under-Fives* ed. Sara & Stephen Corrin, Young Puffin

Diana Ross, 'The Little Red Engine', in *More Stories for Under-Fives* ed. Sara & Stephen Corrin, Young Puffin

Barbara Softly, *Ponder & William* stories, Puffin, o.p.

'The Three Bears', in Anne Rockwell's *The Three Bears and 15 Other Stories*, Hamish Hamilton / Puffin, and in Virginia Haviland's *Fairy Tale Treasury*, Hamish Hamilton / Picture Puffin

Elfrida Vipont & Raymond Briggs, *The Elephant and the Bad Baby*, Hamish Hamilton / Picture Puffin

Brian Wildsmith, *Wild Animals*, Oxford University Press

4

What Shall I Tell?

Stories for Five-
to Twelve-year-olds

This chapter deals with storytimes for two age groups: the fives-to-sevens and the eights-to-twelves. Both groups enjoy the same kinds of stories – folk tales and fantasy, hero tales, adventure, stories about animals and funny stories. Inevitably the two groups overlap, as children vary greatly in their ability to concentrate and appreciate. It is impossible, therefore, to say dogmatically that a particular story will only appeal to children of a certain age.

Children's reactions to a story are determined by the way it is presented, and this is largely a matter of experience. A story you might think of using with an older group can often be told more simply for young children. However, it is usually a question of choosing stories that are younger in content – Robin Hood rather than King Arthur, Ursula Moray Williams's 'The Good Little Christmas Tree' (which has the feeling of a fairy tale and includes much repetition) rather than the Breton legend, 'Brother Johannick and his Silver Bell' (which is more mature and has a religious background). Alison Uttley's tales of magic and enchantment are suitable for older children, while her 'Sam Pig' and 'Tim Rabbit' stories appeal to the younger ones.

It should be remembered that the fives-to-sevens include children who have recently had their first experience of school. When a young child goes to school, his taste and appreciation of stories begins to widen. Gradually his span of attention lengthens and his comprehension develops. He finds new interests and confidence yet at the same time needs the reassurance of hearing familiar stories he associates with infancy. While he can still enjoy 'The Three Bears' and other nursery tales, he now appreciates a longer and more robust story from Grimm, or Andersen's 'The Tinderbox', for example. He still enjoys a picture book but it should have a longer, more mature text. Charles Keeping's *Charley, Charlotte and the Golden Canary*, the story of two friends who are separated by the demolition of their homes and find each other again through a 'golden' canary, or Edward Ardizzone's 'Tim' stories, are both suitable choices.

These younger children appreciate a simple ceremony to begin their story-session. I would recommend something along the lines of that once used in the New York Public Library. A candle is lit as a sign that the story is about to begin, and at the end of the session the youngest child blows it out while all make a secret wish.

It is a good idea to start the session with a picture book, followed by a story without pictures, such as Paul Biegel's *The King of the Copper Mountains*, in which a beloved old king is kept alive by his interest in the intriguing stories told by his friends, the animals, until a magic herb can be brought to cure him. In between the stories there is time for a poem or two from Robert Louis Stevenson's *A Child's Garden of Verses* or Barbara Ireson's *Rhyme Time*. Half an hour is long enough for this younger age group.

An opening ceremony is unnecessary for the eights-to-twelves, but in a regularly held session I suggest you welcome newcomers. A group of children of this age offers the opportunity to tell a wide variety of stories, particularly if the group meets regularly over a period of time. A season of stories can follow a theme to help with continuity – animal stories, hero tales, tales of magic or folk tales from different cultures. A thirty- to forty-minute storytime for this age group might include:

– a Greek legend, 'The Gorgon's Head'

31

- a French Canadian story, 'The Golden Phoenix' by Marius Barbeau
- an extra, to laugh at, Richard Hughes's 'The Elephant's Picnic'

Between the stories try introducing a poem. You will find plenty of suitable examples in *Figgie Hobbin*, Charles Causley's hilarious and moving collection, or in Leila Berg's selection of poetry about animals, *Four Feet and Two*. I have often used poems by Ian Serraillier, Eleanor Farjeon, and James Reeves.

Now to consider in more detail the varied kinds of stories suitable for the two age groups.

Of all the kinds of stories told by storytellers fairy tales are the richest source. What do we mean by fairy stories? Not just 'them made-up things . . . little buzzflies with butterfly wings and gauze petticoats, and shiny stars in their hair' – we would agree with Kipling's Puck that their day is past. Modern children prefer more robust material, but they still enjoy stories of magic with fairy-tale patterns. I remember a *Jackanory* story-writing competition which drew more than six thousand entries, and by far the largest proportion had fairy-tale themes and treatments.

Psychologists say that fairy tales are necessary to a child's development and give form and substance to his imaginings. In them he finds vicarious adventure, danger and conflict, joy and sorrow, good and evil, life and death. These basic and constant patterns appeal to the insecure child who knows that the third and weakest son will triumph; the dragon or the loathly monster will always be destroyed, the good be victorious.

Fairy tales have all the components of ideal stories for telling; they are direct, there is plenty of action, the instruments of magic are familiar things, the settings are natural – mountains, forests, rivers and lakes. There are several distinct types of fairy tales for the storyteller to choose from. For five- to seven-year-olds there are cumulative tales like 'The Old Woman and Her Pig' or 'Henny-Penny'. For seven- to ten-year-olds there are the 'drolls', down-to-earth

32

stories of simple people typified by the world-famous tale 'The Man Who Thought He Could Keep House Better Than His Wife' (Wanda Gág's version, *Gone is Gone*, is very effective for telling) or 'The Three Sillies', which, with its repetitive phrase and ridiculous situations, inevitably makes the audience laugh.

For most children, tales of magic are the favourites, from 'Cinderella', that ancient tale of which there are so many variants, to the homely 'The Elves and the Shoemaker'. Witches are always popular, for they give half-fearful pleasure and can be overcome by brave and clever children like 'the little girl with a kind heart' in Arthur Ransome's 'Baba Yaga'. Today there are many tales of 'good' witches, but to children the only good witch is a bad one. Good witches – or tame dragons – are disappointing, for children want naughty children and bad villains in stories as a substitute for their own misbehaviour. Hence the attraction of Christianna Brand's *Nurse Matilda* and my own *Bad Boys*.

The number of collections of fairy stories available today is enormous. Almost every country in the world is represented, each with its national characteristics but often with similar basic themes. Collections of this kind can be found in abundance on library shelves, but every storyteller should own copies of the standard collections – Joseph Jacobs's *English Fairy Tales*, Andersen and Grimm and some version of Perrault. Katharine Briggs's *Abbey Lubbers, Banshees and Boggarts: A Who's Who of Fairies* is a fascinating source book.

Talking animals figure largely in children's traditional stories – 'The Three Billy-goats Gruff' and 'The Three Pigs' for younger children, for instance, and the 'Brer Rabbit' stories or the West Indian 'Anancy' tales for older children.

33

A good source is Kathleen Arnott's *Animal Folk Tales Around the World*.

Illustrated versions of fables provide excellent material for five- to seven-year-olds. The best-known fables are attributed to Aesop, and La Fontaine included many of them in his classic collection. These brief dramatic stories lend themselves readily to imaginative expansion, for example, 'The Town Mouse and the Country Mouse', 'The Wind and the Sun' and 'The Miller, His Son and their Donkey'.

Greek and Roman myths are often sadly neglected today, yet without some knowledge of them, children will miss many allusions in literature and art. The stories of Ceres and Persephone, of Icarus falling through the sky, his wings singed by his daring flight to the sun, of Midas and the Golden Touch or of Bellerophon and the taming of the winged horse, will remain in children's minds and are an invaluable stimulus to the imagination. Children may not understand the allegory and symbolism of such tales, but they will be enchanted by the stories themselves. There are many versions of the myths, each with its differences in choice of words, complexity, emphasis and angles of approach. Readers interested in myths and other traditional material will find a thoughtful and detailed analysis in Elizabeth Cook's *The Ordinary and the Fabulous*. Myths are not suitable for the younger age group but can well be used with eight- to ten-year-olds; their imagery and romance often have great appeal for teenagers, too. Do not present them as classical tales of long ago, a school subject for study, but tell tnem as *stories* to be enjoyed like any other tales for their own sake.

Similarly, it is worth introducing the absorbing adventures of Odysseus to ten- to twelve-year-olds. The stories of his fight with the one-eyed giant Polyphemus, his encounter with the sorceress Circe and with the Sirens, and his dramatic return home to confront his wife's suitors, often prove highly popular with this age group.

The Norse myths are in a more heroic mood. They are concerned with the larger-than-life relationship between the gods of Asgard, men in Midgard, the Giants in Jotunheim and the 'multitudinous dead' in Niflheim. Gods and men are threatened by the inexorable approach of Ragnarok, day of doom, when all will be destroyed. Stories which appeal to older children are 'The Apples of Iduna', 'How Odin Lost His Eye', and in particular 'The Death of Baldur'. Useful collections are Roger Lancelyn Green's *Myths of the Norsemen* and Kevin Crossley-Holland's *The Faber Book of Northern Legends*.

Norse sagas tell of heroic achievements by people who, although beset by gods and men, show immense courage and endurance. Heroism, loyalty, death rather than dishonour, are the principles that rule the lives of these legendary Norsemen, and there is sweep and excitement in the stories about them. The thirteenth-century Icelandic stories of Grettir the Strong, an outlawed hero who suffered many misfortunes and fought his foes courageously, and of Njal, a wise and brave man who, because of a blood feud, tragically lost his life, are both good, stirring adventure stories for older children.

Ireland has always been the land of storytelling and of legendary heroes, the two most famous being Cuchulain and Finn Mac Cool. The legends surrounding them are complex and compassionate, a blend of folklore, hero tales and romance. Many are too violent and full of 'battle frenzy' to offer to children, but both Cuchulain and Finn personify youth and wild courage and as such have great appeal for the over-tens. The so-called 'three sorrows of storytelling', which include the story of 'The Children of Lir', who were changed into swans by their wicked stepmother and condemned to sail the seas for a thousand years, form an introduction to these cycles. Another very popular story is that of 'Oisin the Harpist and Niahm of the Golden Hair', who rode away to Tir-na-Og, the Land of the Ever Young, on a white horse – 'and those who watched from the green land saw them no more'.

All children should know something about the legends of King Arthur and his Knights of the Round Table. Their complexity and subject matter mean that their appeal is largely to children of about twelve, although Gwyn Jones's

35

'Where Arthur Sleeps' is a fine dramatic tale suitable for eight- to ten-year-olds. I have found the most popular stories from the cycle to be the drawing of the sword Excalibur, Merlin's spells and the passing of Arthur. Roger Lancelyn Green's *King Arthur and His Knights of the Round Table* is a useful retelling. Interspersing an occasional quotation from Tennyson's *Idylls of the King* helps to build up the atmosphere. The story of the quest for the Holy Grail is complicated, but fortunately there is a beautiful and succinct retelling in Rosemary Sutcliff's *The Light Beyond the Forest*.

Among other enjoyable hero tales a favourite is that of the friendship between Roland and Oliver, both Paladins of Charlemagne, whose tragic end at Roncesvalles is told by Ian Serraillier in *The Ivory Horn*. Every country has a national hero around whose exploits legends have gathered, to become a rich source of stories.

Younger children are fascinated by England's legendary national hero, Robin Hood, helped by the highly romantic-ized versions on television and in films. Robin Hood's championship of the poor and weak and the tricks he plays on those in authority have won him an enduring place in the affections of children. Most of the stories originated in ballads but they are best told in longer, prose form.

Ballads are close neighbours to hero tales. They recount heroic deeds and romantic encounters, whether legendary or historically based, from 'Sir Patrick Spens' to 'Tamlane' to the tragic tale 'Binoorie':

> She clasped her hands about a broom root,
> *Binoorie, O Binoorie*;
> But her cruel sister she loosed them out,
> By the bonnie mill-dams of Binoorie.

Grace Hallworth, the well-known storyteller, has tried chanting the ballad to chords on an auto-harp, thus reproducing the way ballads were originally presented. Some teachers and librarians use a guitar to accompany more modern ballads to great effect.

'Tall tales', that is, stories in which the bounds of

probability are stretched so far that the story becomes extravagant, entertaining nonsense, are seldom used with children although their humour is often a success with ten- and eleven-year-olds. The classic examples are R. E. Raspe's tales of the exploits of Baron Munchausen, published in 1785. Here we read of one hunter whose dog literally ran its legs off in the service of its master and so became a dachshund, and another who shot a stag out of whose head a cherry tree was growing laden with fruit, so he had cherry pie for supper.

The modern examples of the tall tale come from America and are stories of fabulous heroes. Paul Bunyan stories are typical: his ox measured 'forty-two axe-handles and a plug of chewing tobacco from tip to tip of its horns', and his hunters were so tall that they had to stand on ladders to shave themselves. Such tales are perhaps a natural product of the exuberance of the early frontiersmen and hunters in their new land. Examples can be found in Virginia Haviland's *North American Legends*.

Although fairy tales and fantasies of various kinds are the major source of stories for telling, some children prefer more realistic tales. For one child a broom is a witch's steed, for another it is something to sweep the floor with. The story-teller's repertoire must always include stories for the child who poses that awkward question, 'But is it true? Did it really happen?' Such children identify with boys and girls, heroes and heroines, who *do* something, who meet danger and

37

achieve goals that are possible in what is called the 'real world'. Young children enjoy Astrid Lindgren's stories of a natural and homely family in *The Bullerby Children*. The older group usually like the story of a boy marooned by a snowstorm with Zlateh the goat, by Isaac Bashevis Singer, or a shortened version of *The Boy Who Was Afraid* by Armstrong Sperry, the story of a South Seas boy's fear of the sea. John Masefield's *Jim Davis*, an exciting smuggling story, can be told as a serial, while E. Nesbit's stories are rich in amusing episodes which can be told singly. For eleven- to twelve-year-olds there are short stories like Bill Naughton's collection *The Goalkeeper's Revenge*, in which there is a tragic story of Spit Nolan, champion trolley-rider, who loses both the race and his life. From the realistic but fictitious story it is a natural step to true stories of exploration, natural disasters and real people – Captain Scott, Madame Curie, Mozart, Amy Johnson, Hans C. Andersen – anyone whose life makes a good story and about whom you, the storyteller, can feel enthusiasm.

Humorous stories should not be forgotten, as everyone likes to laugh. Such stories are welcome after the main story in a storytelling session, providing an opportunity to relax. With young children try Joan Aiken's *Tales of Arabel's Raven*, a bird who has the awkward habit of shouting 'Nevermore' down telephones, or Rose Fyleman's 'The Magic Umbrella'. With older boys and girls try a story from J.B.S. Haldane's *My Friend Mr Leakey* (a magician), Norman Hunter's 'Professor Branestawm' books, or an episode from the amusing *The Phoenix and the Carpet* by E. Nesbit. Nonsense poems add spice – Edward Lear's verses, Belloc's *Cautionary Tales*, Spike Milligan's *Silly Verse for Kids*.

Lastly there are what I call 'granny stories', an older person's reminiscences about his or her life and experiences. These have real value in bridging the generations and giving a child a sense of the continuity of time, always a difficult concept for young children. One father beginning a story with 'When I was a little boy' was somewhat disconcerted when his young son said sagely, 'Oh yes, when there were dinosaurs . . . '

The main question we should always ask ourselves when selecting is: 'What is it in this story that I want to share with children? Is it fun, beauty, excitement, interest in other people, an underlying principle worthy of emulation?' Unless a story has some quality worth sharing, it is not worth telling.

No one can say what makes one particular story *yours*, but I have found that suddenly a story leaps from the page and is alive and full of meaning for me. I know that it is *my* story and that I shall be able to tell it with conviction. This must have been the experience of every storyteller. By reading and telling, trial and error, the storyteller gradually develops a sixth sense. In time you will *know* that a story is right for you as soon as you see it. When a story is yours in this way, it is reasonable to expect that it will please children too, because you believe in it and can tell it with enthusiasm.

BOOKS & STORIES MENTIONED

Aesop, *The Best of Aesop's Fables* retold by Margaret Clark, Walker; in *The Faber Storybook* by Kathleen Lines, Faber; in *Tomie de Paola's Favourite Nursery Tales*, Methuen

Joan Aiken, *Tales of Arabel's Raven*, Cape / BBC Books

Hans C. Andersen, 'The Tinderbox', in Erik Haugaard's *Hans Andersen – His Classic Fairy Tales*, Gollancz

Anancy stories. In *Anancy-Spiderman* by James Berry, Walker

'The Apples of Iduna', in Kevin Crossley-Holland's *Faber Book of Northern Legends* and in Kathleen Lines's *The Faber Storybook*, both Faber

Edward Ardizzone, *Little Tim and the Brave Sea Captain*, Picture Puffin; *Ship's Cook Ginger*, Picturemac; *Tim All Alone, Tim and Charlotte, Tim and Ginger, Tim in Danger, Tim to the Lighthouse, Tim's Friend Towser* and *Tim's Last Voyage*, all Oxford University Press

Kathleen Arnott, *African Myths and Legends*, Oxford University Press

Kathleen Arnott, *Animal Folk Tales Around the World*, Blackie, o.p.

Marius Barbeau, 'The Golden Phoenix', in *A Second Storyteller's Choice* ed. Eileen Colwell, Bodley Head, o.p.

'Bellerophon', in *The Faber Storybook* by Kathleen Lines, Faber
Hilaire Belloc, *Selected Cautionary Verses*, Puffin
Leila Berg, *Four Feet and Two*, Puffin, o.p.
Paul Biegel, *King of the Copper Mountains*, Young Lion
Christianna Brand, *Nurse Matilda*, Swift / Knight
Brer Rabbit. In *Tales of Uncle Remus: The Adventures of Brer Rabbit* by
   Julius Lester, Bodley Head / Pan
Katharine Briggs, *Abbey Lubbers, Banshees and Boggarts*, Kestrel, o.p.
'Brother Johannick and his Silver Bell' by Elizabeth Clark, in *The
   Puffin Book of Christmas Stories* ed. Sara & Stephen Corrin, Puffin
Paul Bunyan, 'Babe the Blue Ox', in Virginia Haviland's *The Faber
   Book of North American Legends*, Faber
Charles Causley, *Figgie Hobbin*, Macmillan / Puffin
'Ceres and Persephone', in *Stories from Ancient Greece* by Pamela
   Oldfield, Kingfisher; in *Stories for Seven-Year-Olds* ed. Sara &
   Stephen Corrin, Faber / Puffin
'The Children of Lir', in *Druids, Gods & Heroes from Celtic Mythology*
   by A. Ross, Peter Lowe
'Cinderella', two picture books: Paul Galdone, World's Work, and
   Fiona French, Oxford University Press; and in *The Faber Book of
   Favourite Fairy Tales* ed. Sara & Stephen Corrin, Faber
Eileen Colwell, *Bad Boys*, Young Puffin
Elizabeth Cook, *The Ordinary and the Fabulous*, Cambridge
   University Press, o.p.
Cuchulain. In *Cuchulain: Hound of Ulster* by R.J. Stewart, Firebird
'The Death of Baldur', in *Myths of the Norsemen* by R.L. Green,
   Puffin
'The Elves and the Shoemaker', in *The Three Bears and 15 Other
   Stories* by Anne Rockwell, Hamish Hamilton / Puffin; in *Tomie
   dePaola's Favourite Nursery Tales*, Methuen, and in Cynthia &
   William Birrer's picture book, *The Shoemaker and the Elves*, Hippo
Eleanor Farjeon, in Eleanor Graham's *A Puffin Quartet of Poets*,
   Puffin
'Finn MacCool', in Kathleen Lines's *The Faber Storybook*, Faber; in
   Barbara Ker Wilson's *Scottish Folk-tales and Legends*, Oxford
   University Press; in Rosemary Sutcliff's *High Deeds of Finn
   MacCool*, Puffin
Rose Fyleman, 'The Magic Umbrella', in *More Stories for Under-
   Fives* ed. Sara & Stephen Corrin, Puffin
Wanda Gág, *Gone is Gone*, in Virginia Haviland's *Fairy Tale
   Treasury*, Hamish Hamilton / Puffin

'The Gorgon's Head', in *The Kingfisher Book of Myths and Legends* by Anthony Horowitz, Kingfisher

Roger L. Green, 'Merlin's Spells, Excalibur, The Passing of Arthur' in *King Arthur and His Knights of the Round Table*, Puffin

The Brothers Grimm: Popular Folk Tales, trans. Brian Alderson, Gollancz, and *Grimms' Fairy Tales*, trans. Peter Carter, Oxford University Press

J.B.S. Haldane, 'My Friend Mr Leakey', in *I Like This Story* by Kaye Webb, Kestrel / Puffin

Virginia Haviland, *The Faber Book of North American Legends*, Faber

'Henny Penny', in *The Three Bears and 15 Other Stories* by Anne Rockwell, Hamish Hamilton / Puffin

Norman Hunter, *The Incredible Adventures of Professor Branestawm*, Bodley Head / Puffin

'How Odin Lost His Eye', in R.L. Green's *Myths of the Norsemen*, Puffin, and in Kathleen Lines's *The Faber Storybook*, Faber

Richard Hughes, 'The Elephant's Picnic', in *Don't Blame Me*, Chatto & Windus, and in Sara & Stephen Corrin's *Laugh Out Loud*, Faber

'Icarus', in *Stories from Ancient Greece* by Pamela Oldfield, Kingfisher

Barbara Ireson, *Rhyme Time 1* and *Rhyme Time 2*, both Beaver

Joseph Jacobs, *English Fairy Tales*, Dover; selection in Puffin

Gwyn Jones, 'Where Arthur Sleeps', in *Welsh Legends and Folk-Tales*, Puffin

Charles Keeping, *Charley, Charlotte and the Golden Canary*, Oxford University Press, o.p.

King Arthur. In *The New Golden Land Anthology* ed. Judith Elkin, Viking Kestrel / Puffin; R.L. Green, *King Arthur and His Knights of the Round Table*, Puffin

'King Midas', in Pamela Oldfield's *Stories from Ancient Greece*, Kingfisher; in Sara & Stephen Corrin's *The Faber Book of Favourite Fairy Tales*, Faber; and in Nancy & Edward Blishen's *A Treasury of Stories for Seven-Year-Olds*, Kingfisher

La Fontaine. Picture books by Brian Wildsmith: *The Hare and the Tortoise, The Lion and the Rat, The Miller, the Boy and the Donkey, The North Wind and the Sun, The Rich Man and the Shoemaker*, all Oxford University Press

Edward Lear, *The Complete Nonsense of Edward Lear*, Faber; Brian Alderson's *A Book of Bosh*, Puffin

Astrid Lindgren, *All about the Bullerby Children*, Methuen

'The Man Who Thought He Could Keep House Better Than His Wife', in *My First Big Storybook* by Richard Bamberger, Young Puffin

John Masefield, *Jim Davis*, Puffin, o.p.

The Miller, his Son and their Donkey, picture book by Eugen Sopko, Abelard/North-South; *The Miller, the Boy and the Donkey* picture book by Brian Wildsmith, Oxford University Press

Spike Milligan, *Silly Verse for Kids*, Puffin

Bill Naughton, *The Goalkeeper's Revenge*, Puffin

E. Nesbit, *The Phoenix and the Carpet*, Puffin

Norse Myths. *Northern Lights: Legends, Sagas and Folk-Tales* by Kevin Crossley-Holland, Faber

'Odysseus', in *Tales of the Greek Heroes* by R. L. Green, Puffin

'Oisin the Harpist and Niahm of the Golden Hair', in *The High Deeds of Finn MacCool* by Rosemary Sutcliff, Puffin

'The Old Woman and Her Pig', in *The Fairy Tale Treasury* by Virginia Haviland, Hamish Hamilton / Picture Puffin; Priscilla Lamont's picture book *The Troublesome Pig*, Hamish Hamilton / Picture Piper

Charles Perrault, *Sleeping Beauty and Other Favourite Fairy Tales*, trans. Angela Carter, Gollancz

Arthur Ransome, 'Baba Yaga', in *Old Peter's Russian Tales*, Cape / Puffin

R.E. Raspe, *Baron Munchausen*, Methuen

James Reeves, in Eleanor Graham's *A Puffin Quartet of Poets*, Puffin; also *Ragged Robin*, Walker, and *The Wandering Moon & Other Poems*, Puffin

Robin Hood. In R.L. Green's *Adventures of Robin Hood*, Puffin, and in *The Chronicles of Robin Hood* by Rosemary Sutcliff, Oxford University Press, o.p.

'Roland and Oliver'. In Maurice Saxby's *The Great Deeds of Superheroes*, Dragon's World

Ian Serraillier, in Eleanor Graham's *A Puffin Quartet of Poets*, Puffin

Ian Serraillier, *The Ivory Horn*, Oxford University Press, o.p.

Isaac B. Singer, *Zlateh the Goat*, Kestrel

Armstrong Sperry, *The Boy Who Was Afraid*, Heinemann Educational

Robert L. Stevenson, *A Child's Garden of Verses*, illustrated by Brian Wildsmith, Oxford University Press; illustrated by Michael Foreman, Gollancz; illustrated by Eve Garnett, Puffin

Rosemary Sutcliff, 'Excalibur', 'Merlin's Spells', in *The Light Beyond the Forest*, Knight

Rosemary Sutcliff, 'The Passing of Arthur', *The Road to Camlann*, Knight

'Ballad of Tamlane', in Kevin Crossley-Holland's *British Folk Tales*, Orchard, and in Barbara Ker Wilson's *Scottish Folk-tales and Legends*, Oxford University Press

'The Three Bears', 'The Three Billy Goats Gruff' and 'The Three Pigs', all in Anne Rockwell's *The Three Bears and 15 Other Stories*, Hamish Hamilton / Puffin

'The Three Sillies', in Joseph Jacobs's *English Fairy Tales*, Dover or Puffin; in Sara & Stephen Corrin's *Faber Book of Favourite Fairy Tales*, Faber, and *Stories for Seven-Year-Olds*, Faber / Puffin

'The Town Mouse and the Country Mouse', in Margaret Clark's *The Best of Aesop's Fables*, Walker; *The Tale of Johnny Town-Mouse* by Beatrix Potter, Warne

Alison Uttley, *Sam Pig* stories, Faber; *Sam Pig Goes to the Seaside*, Young Puffin

Alison Uttley, *The Adventures of Tim Rabbit*, Young Puffin

Ursula Moray Williams, 'The Good Little Christmas Tree', in *Tell Me Another Story*, ed. Eileen Colwell, Young Puffin, and separately in an edition illustrated by Gillian Tyler, Julia MacRae

The Wind and the Sun, Brian Wildsmith's picture book, Oxford University Press

Additional suggestions

Family stories: Martin Waddell's *Tales from the Shop That Never Shuts* (Puffin); Dick King-Smith's *Friends and Brothers* (Heinemann / Mammoth); Berlie Doherty's *How Green You Are* (Methuen / Lions); Laura Ingalls Wilder's *Little House in the Big Woods* (Methuen / Puffin).

Humorous stories: Jeff Brown's *Flat Stanley* (Methuen); Florence Parry Heide's *The Shrinking of Treehorn* (Young Puffin); James Howe's *Bunnicula* (Young Lions); Maggie Pearson's *Silly Tilly* (Hodder & Stoughton)

5

Adapting the Story for Telling

Sometimes you will find that an otherwise suitable story is difficult to tell as it stands. A story for telling needs a different construction and emphasis from a story written for reading to yourself. Added to this, most stories need to be modified to suit a particular audience or age group. Experience shows that some adaptation is both legitimate and desirable.

The most common adaptation is the shortening of a lengthy story to meet the limitations of time or the powers of concentration of a particular age group. To try to pack too much into the time available gives a feeling of haste – storytelling should always be unhurried and relaxed – and may mean that the climax cannot be given its due impact. Usually a reasonable shortening is quite possible without spoiling the story as a whole; indeed, most published stories benefit from a little pruning.

One of the most obvious ways of doing this is to remove secondary ramifications of the plot, which should also help to keep the storyline clear. A good example is 'Volkh's Journey to the East' by E.M. Almedingen. The main plot concerns Volkh's wishes and the way they help him to win a seat among the Knights of the Golden Table, but at the very beginning of the story there is a secondary plot about Volkh's mother and her most treasured possession. This has no significance for the main plot and can be omitted without spoiling the story. Another example is the Polish folk tale, 'The Jolly Tailor Who Became King'. It contains a strange piece of folklore about the tailor's visit to the devil's house, which will mean little to children. This can be omitted, for the story is complete, and indeed more suitable for children, without it. A brief analysis of the plot of any story will soon make it obvious when such asides can safely be discarded.

Unnecessarily detailed descriptive passages not only slow down the action, they also leave little scope for the child's imagination to come into play. One of the benefits of storytelling is that it provides a stimulus to the imagination; this is lost if every scene and person is described, as they would be in a film or on television. An adult's description of a princess, for instance, will probably fall far short of the child's own glamorous picture. A scene needs only a general description for the child to identify it with some place known to her and so visualize it to her own satisfaction. When reading to yourself, you can skip or read long descriptive passages as you wish, but they cannot be ignored in a told story and may only bore or confuse the listener. Take this from the beginning of Walter de la Mare's story, 'The Three Sleeping Boys of Warwickshire':

> In a low-ceiled, white-washed room on the uppermost floor of a red-brick building in Pleasant Street, Cheriton, standing there in their glazed cases, is a collection of shells, conches, sea-weeds, dried salty sea flowers, fossils, staring birds, goggling fish with glass eyes . . .

A child might well be forgiven for asking 'When are you going to begin the story?'

Sometimes a rearrangement of the sequence of events may be justified for the sake of clarity, or even the addition of an event which has been implied but not told. In the original version of Rose Fyleman's 'The Magic Umbrella', the old woman's sudden flight to the top of the church steeple is only mentioned as a possibility. So many children asked 'But why hasn't she gone to the top of the steeple?' that I was forced to add this crowning absurdity in my own words; this has become an essential part of the story in all subsequent tellings.

45

Whatever else is deleted, repetitive phrases must be retained because they are attractive to children and invite participation. How much tamer the story of 'The Gingerbread Man' would be if it lacked the refrain, 'Run, run, as fast as you can, You can't catch me, I'm the Gingerbread Man' – children can never resist joining in with gusto. Would the story of 'The Three Pigs' have had the same appeal if the sinister Wolf had never growled, 'Then I'll huff and I'll puff and I'll blow your house down'? There is no doubt that the popularity of the story of Henny-Penny is largely due to the repetition of the names of her companions: Cocky-locky, Ducky-daddles, Goosey-poosey, Turkey-lurkey and the villainous Foxy-woxy.

The opening is all-important in the telling of a story. Most stories, particularly folk tales, begin with some variant of 'Once upon a time', a phrase that establishes the outside-time of the story, a magic faraway time in which anything can happen. The first few sentences should always give some indication of what the story is going to be about:

> There was once a poor widow who had an only son named Jack, and a cow named Milky-white, and she was their only fortune . . .

This kind of down-to-earth opening is characteristic of most folk tales. Even better, however, is a first sentence that excites a child's expectations of what is to come. Take this from Andersen's 'The Tinderbox':

> A soldier came marching along the high road, right, left! right, left! He had his knapsack on his back and a sword by his side, for he had been to the wars and was now returning home. And on the road he met an old witch – a horrid-looking creature she was . . .

Or this intriguing opening from a Russian fairy tale, 'To Your Good Health':

> Long, long ago there lived a king who was such a mighty

46

monarch **that** whenever he sneezed everyone in the whole country had to say 'To your good health!' Everyone said it except the shepherd with the bright blue eyes, and he would *not* say it . . .

First sentences are not always the best introductions, for the author may never have had the experience of telling a story to a group of restless children. It may be necessary, therefore, to write your own first sentence. If so, make it as arresting as you can and commit it to memory so firmly that you can confidently get over that apprehensive moment before the story is properly under way.

Equally important for success is the *last* sentence because it is largely responsible for the final impression left in the child's mind. It must fit the story, leaving no ragged ends. Whether it is tragic or comic, the listening child should feel satisfied that all is well, the quest completed, the evil conquered, the 'good' characters living happily ever after:

Out of the bag jumped little Dog Turpie and he ate up all the Hobyahs. And that is why there are no Hobyahs left anywhere in the world.

Such reassurance is very important for little children.

The Hungarian tale of 'The Witch and the Swan Maiden' has a similarly reassuring ending which is likely to appeal to older children:

The witch filled the room with darkness: the people sat and shuddered in the darkness; the king and queen clung together; and when the darkness lifted, the witch had vanished.

So the king, the queen and the little prince lived in great happiness ever after.

But an ending like the one from Andersen's 'The Little Mermaid' is too vague and descriptive to be really satisfactory:

47

We fly invisibly through the dwellings of men, where there are no children: and whenever we find a good child, who gives pleasure to his parents and deserves their love, the good God shortens our time of probation . . .

You should always try to convey a feeling of finality at the end of a story, and this can often be achieved by intonation alone. At other times a slight rephrasing or transposing of words is effective. As an example, consider this from Patrick Chalmers's 'The Little Pagan Faun':

Now *you* mayn't be able to believe that the Lady promised the little pagan faun anything of the sort, but *I* can assure you that she did, and that he trotted off into the woods again, munching his cake and feeling much comforted about things, just as the clocks were striking twelve and it was Christmas Day.

This is too wordy and does not have the impact and finality the story needs. The important thing to remember is that the little pagan faun is comforted and that it is Christmas. My solution was:

So the little pagan faun trotted off into the woods again, munching his cake and feeling much comforted. At that very moment the clocks struck twelve. It was CHRISTMAS DAY!

Endings should always be brief and to the point, for once the climax has been reached, children tend to lose interest.

Some details in traditional material may seem too gruesome for children and, if so, they should be omitted or toned down. The gory fights between Beowulf and the monster Grendel in the Anglo-Saxon epic poem, or the 'battle frenzies' in the Irish hero stories, are very often disturbing, and many folk tales are strewn with blood-curdling episodes. One of the most gruesome is 'Mr Fox': when Lady Mary goes into Mr Fox's, her fiancé's, house she sees: 'bodies and skeletons of beautiful young ladies all stained with blood . . .

The sword cut off the hand, which jumped up into the air, and fell of all places in the world into Lady Mary's lap.' More subtle but peculiarly chilling is Andersen's 'The Red Shoes', in which a vain girl who goes to her confirmation wearing red shoes is condemned to dance the world over until 'she is pale and cold and her skin shrinks and crumples up like a skeleton's'. Although the executioner cuts off her feet, the red shoes dance on.

Some children may gloat over such details, but this is generally mere bravado. With an audience of young children in mind, it may be as well to avoid such endings as the version of 'Cinderella' where the ugly sisters' eyes are plucked out by pigeons, or Perrault's retelling of 'The Sleeping Beauty', in which the princess's mother-in-law plans to eat her own grandchildren.

However, you should beware of being too guarded: children often seem to accept punishments at the end of traditional folk tales as being well deserved and do not visualize them in all their horror as an adult might. Certainly, stories which feature dragons or other monsters having their heads cut off do not usually upset children, as long as such punishments are mentioned matter-of-factly and not enlarged upon. They are on a par with the Queen of Hearts' 'Off with their heads!'

Can we – and ought we to – introduce a book we want children to read by telling a part of it freely? I dislike 'retold' classics which reduce a book notable for its style to a rehash of what is possibly not a very good plot. Dickens and the Brontës, who are the most common victims of this process, did not write for children, and their books are probably best saved until the child can read them for himself. But when the book in question *was* intended for children yet presents difficulties to young readers, there may be a case for adapting it to make it more accessible. A prime example is *The Water Babies*; the story of the little chimney sweep who becomes a water baby has appeal, but the style is overloaded with period verbiage and moral reflections, which can be offputting. Try retelling the first part; your audience may be inspired to attempt the rest of the book on their own. Similarly E.

49

Nesbit's books are well worth introducing for their comedy and characters; an episode from *The Phoenix and the Carpet* never fails to entertain.

An interesting problem is what to do with stories told in the first person. Eleanor Farjeon's story of 'Bertha Goldfoot' is told by an old nurse; Masefield's smuggling story, *Jim Davis*, by a boy of fourteen or so; J.B.S. Haldane's 'A Meal with a Magician' by an unknown young man. The storyteller is unlikely to resemble any of these people, so is it incongruous to tell these stories from the point of view of their protagonists? Will the suggestion that the story is happening get in the way of the child's own identification with the hero or heroine? It may seem wiser to tell such stories in reported speech, but this decision must be made afresh for each story of this kind. 'A Meal with a Magician', for instance, undoubtedly gains impact and authenticity by being told as a personal experience, especially as the narrator is largely anonymous and all attention is focused on the remarkable happenings. After telling this amusing story in the first person, I have had children ask me, as Mr Leakey's friend, to tell them where he lived so that they could go there and perhaps catch a glimpse of Pompey the dragon or Oliver the octopus.

To sum up: for telling, a story must have a pattern that comprises an inviting beginning, not too many characters, a logical series of events (that is, not a series of arbitrary events that have little connection with each other), plenty of action, and a satisfying ending. The story should build to a climax quickly followed by the ending. One of the most lively storytellers, John Masefield, said,

> Remarkable openings, proper pauses, notable climaxes, make a good story.

An example of such a pattern is Andersen's 'The Real Princess'. Brief as it is, there is an intriguing beginning with a prince searching for a real princess; the arrival of a girl in a dramatic storm who, in spite of appearances, claims that she is a real princess; the ingenious test the queen sets for her, and the triumphant climax when the princess proves her royal status by feeling a pea through a mountain of mattresses and eiderdowns. The classic happy ending is followed by the sentence which establishes the authenticity of the story: the actual pea may be seen in the royal museum.

Even after subsequent retellings when you have established the pattern of the story and its details, you will find that further changes have crept into the story, almost without your knowledge, as a result of the reaction of the audience. An extra minor character has been introduced, another character has disappeared, details have been added or omitted, frightening incidents have been toned down for the sake of some sensitive child. Whatever additions and subtractions have been made, the basic story remains the same and keeps its identity. It has merely been shaped by the storyteller and the response of the audience. That is as it should be, and as it has always been.

BOOKS & STORIES MENTIONED

E.M. Almedingen, 'Volkh's Journey to the East', in *Imagine That!*, ed. Sara & Stephen Corrin, Faber / Puffin

Hans C. Andersen, 'The Little Mermaid', 'The Red Shoes', 'The Tinderbox', in Erik Haugaard's *Hans Andersen – His Classic Fairy Tales*, Gollancz

Hans C. Andersen, 'The Princess and the Pea' ('The Real Princess'), in Erik Haugaard's *Hans Andersen – His Classic Fairy Tales*, Gollancz; in Sara & Stephen Corrin's *Faber Book of Favourite Fairy Tales*, Faber; and Margaret Greaves's *The Princess and the Pea*, Methuen

Beowulf. In *The Faber Book of Magical Tales* ed. Kathleen Lines, Faber

Patrick Chalmers, 'The Little Pagan Faun', in *A Storyteller's Choice* ed. Eileen Colwell, Bodley Head, o.p.

'Cinderella', Paul Galdone's picture book, World's Work, and Fiona French's picture book, Oxford University Press; and in *The Faber Book of Favourite Fairy Tales* ed. Sara & Stephen Corrin, Faber

Walter de la Mare, 'The Three Sleeping Boys of Warwickshire', in *The Dutch Cheese and Other Stories*, Puffin

Eleanor Farjeon, 'Bertha Goldfoot', in *The Old Nurse's Stocking Basket*, Oxford University Press / Puffin, o.p.

Rose Fyleman, 'The Magic Umbrella', in *More Stories for Under-Fives* ed. Sara & Stephen Corrin, Puffin

'The Gingerbread Man' in Anne Rockwell's *The Three Bears and 15 Other Stories*, Hamish Hamilton / Puffin

J.B.S. Haldane, 'A Meal with a Magician', in Sara & Stephen Corrin's *Laugh Out Loud*, Faber

'Henny Penny' in Anne Rockwell's *The Three Bears and 15 Other Stories*, Hamish Hamilton / Puffin

'The Hobyahs', in *More English Fairy Tales* by Joseph Jacobs, Dover

'The Jolly Tailor Who Became King' by L.M. Borski, in *A Storyteller's Choice*, ed. Eileen Colwell, Bodley Head, o.p.

Charles Kingsley, *The Water Babies*, Dent / Puffin Classics

John Masefield, *Jim Davis*, Puffin, o.p.

'Mr Fox' in Joseph Jacobs's *English Fairy Tales*, Dover, and in Alan Garner's *Book of British Fairy Tales*, Collins

E. Nesbit, *The Phoenix and the Carpet*, Puffin Classics

'Sleeping Beauty', in *Sleeping Beauty and Other Favourite Fairy Tales* trans. Angela Carter, Gollancz

'The Three Pigs' in Anne Rockwell's *The Three Bears and 15 Other Stories*, Hamish Hamilton / Puffin

'To Your Good Health', from Andrew Lang, in Kathleen Lines's *The Faber Storybook*, Faber

'The Witch and the Swan Maiden', in Ruth Manning-Sanders's *The Glass Man and the Golden Bird*, Oxford University Press, o.p.

6

Remembering the Story

It is seldom necessary to learn a story word for word, and this is particularly true of folk tales. There is no definitive version of these old stories, for until the last century they were handed down by word of mouth. No doubt storytellers in every generation make slight alterations, while always retaining the basic pattern. New versions constantly appear, so the storyteller is free to tell the tales in her own words.

A story learnt by rote is not usually as absorbing for the audience as one told in the storyteller's own words so that it sounds spontaneous. Memorizing sometimes causes self-consciousness, and a story learnt line by line can often sound like a recitation. It is also risky, for any sudden interruption can break the storyteller's concentration and make her forget what she was saying. This is disconcerting, not only for the storyteller but also for the children who find it difficult to pick up the thread of the story again.

Although the keynote of storytelling is spontaneity, this does not mean that the storyteller is improvising – far from it. What it does mean is that the story has become so much a part of yourself that it flows freely. Imagine the basic work of preparation as the trunk of a tree, firmly rooted and very much alive. As the story is absorbed, the tree branches freely and opens naturally into leaves of imagination – but these are still part of the tree itself.

How to set about remembering a story? There are many methods, according to the kind of memory each individual has. Generally speaking, however, there is a basic pattern:

– First, read the story to yourself several times, once for

the story only, then concentrating on its *construction*. Notice how it works up to its climax, how it *feels* as to mood, how it ends.

– Now is the time to jot down an outline of the story, without reference to the text, and the names of the characters as you remember them. The very act of writing these down helps to fix them in the memory. Comparing the outline with the original, you may be surprised to discover what you have missed.

– Studying the story in more detail, make a note of repetitive phrases that are vital to the story and must be retained.

Wanda Gág knew the value of repetition for encouraging children to participate. Her 'Hundreds of cats, thousands of cats, millions and billions and trillions of cats', from *Millions of Cats*, has been chanted by untold numbers of children. Or take a cumulative story like 'The Tale of a Turnip', which in Elizabeth Clark's version runs like this:

. . . and the little Mouse had hold of the little black-and-white Cat, the little black-and-white Cat had hold of the little Girl the grandchild, the little Girl the grandchild had hold of the little old Woman the grandmother, and the little old Woman the grandmother had hold of the little old Man her husband, and the little old Man her husband had hold of the turnip; and they pulled, and they pulled, and they pulled, and *up* came the turnip!

There may also be phrases that help to show character, and these are worth noting down. In 'Tom Tit Tot', for example, the simple daughter says to herself of the pies, ' "Well, if they'll come again, I'll eat 'em now." And she set to work and ate 'em all, first and last.'

As the story begins to take shape in your mind, try to visualize it so that you can see it as a series of colourful, moving pictures. If the storyteller cannot see the story, the audience won't be able to either. Children won't necessarily see the same mental picture as the storyteller, but that does not seem to matter. This was brought home to me when I was telling stories to blind children who could not possibly visualize what was in my mind's eye, yet were obviously content with their imaginings. You have only to think of such an everyday sight as a river to realize how differently it can appear to each of us. In a story each child sees a river he knows and seems right to him. If it were possible to look into each child's imagination when telling a story, we would see an astonishing variety of images.

As an experiment try to visualize a story you know well: Andersen's 'The Nightingale', for instance. Stand with the courtiers and the kitchen maid as they wait in the forest to hear the Nightingale sing. Imagine the scene in the palace as the emperor waits condescendingly for the Nightingale to appear. Look at the artificial Nightingale and listen to its song. What do you see? What do you hear? Building up a mental picture full of sound and colour is a great help in remembering a story.

As we become familiar with a story, the characters develop into real people. Because we know them, their adventures are easier to remember. In 'Epaminondas', the familiar story of the child who 'hasn't got the sense he was born with', so always applies his aunt's sensible suggestions too late, with ludicrous results, each incident is linked to the next so the story is easily memorized. With more complicated stories, the plot can usually be divided into sections so that the logical progress of events is clear and more easily remembered. This approach may seem clinical, but it is only a temporary device to aid the memory.

Now you are ready to tell the story *aloud* to yourself or to anyone who will listen. Some people find it useful to record themselves with a tape recorder. This is the only way to discover the places in the story where the right words don't come 'trippingly on the tongue' and where your memory is failing you. Only when you no longer need to think about the words can you be sure that you really know the story.

Words are to the storyteller what notes of music are to the composer or paint to the artist. Listen to this from Malory's *Morte D'Arthur*:

'Therefore,' said Arthur unto Sir Bedivere, 'take thou Excalibur, my good sword, and go with it to yonder water side, and when thou comest there I charge thee throw my sword in that water, and come again and tell me what thou seest . . . '

Here the choice of words gives a strong sense of period, and even if 'thee' and 'thou' are replaced by 'you', this passage still retains its authentic ring.

Or this, from Wanda Gág's *Gone is Gone*. Here is a different world, the countryside in a folk tale:

The sky was blue, the sun right gay and golden, and the flowers they were like angels' eyes blinking in the grass . . . .

The way words are used plays an important part in establishing the mood of the story. The following passage from Oscar Wilde's 'The Selfish Giant' shows the sudden change from the happy atmosphere of the garden to the threatening return of the Giant:

It was a large and lovely garden with soft green grass. Here and there over the grass stood beautiful flowers like stars, and there were twelve peach-trees that in the spring-time broke out into delicate blossoms of pink and pearl, and in the autumn bore rich fruit. The birds sat on the trees and sang so sweetly that the children used to stop their games in order to listen to them. 'How happy we are here!' they cried to each other.

One day the Giant came back . . .

Should we use slang when telling fairy tales? Is it fitting that a long-ago prince should say 'O.K.' or that Boots should get 'real mad'? To me, this is pantomime language and quite out of place in the magic atmosphere of a fairy tale. Although archaic language is obviously unsuitable for modern children, the storyteller should always be sensitive to the feeling of a story and the words she uses to tell it.

While there is a rich variety of stories that can be told in one's own words, some stories must retain the author's words in their entirety. Kipling's *Just So Stories* are an obvious example. Could any other words be used for 'The Elephant's Child'?

> . . . Before he thought what he was doing he schlooped up a schloop of mud from the banks of the great grey-green, greasy Limpopo, and slapped it on his head, where it made a cool, schloopy-sloshy mudcap all trickly behind his ears.

Similarly, stories beautifully written by masters of their craft should never be reproduced in the storyteller's own, relatively inadequate language. Walter de la Mare, Laurence Housman, Rumer Godden and Eleanor Farjeon are such writers. On the whole, Walter de la Mare's stories are more suitable for reading than telling because of their contemplative style, but his imaginative versions of well-known fairy tales in the collection *Tales Told Again* are well worth telling – in the author's words. The stories are more direct and shorter than most of his work, and their content is familiar. Laurence Housman's collections of short stories include a few that are popular with children, particularly 'A Chinese Fairy Tale', in which an artist steps into his own picture and walks along its painted paths to disappear for three hundred years.

Of Rumer Godden's tales I would recommend *The*

Mousewife, a perfect story inspired by a passage in Dorothy Wordsworth's diary. The mousewife is different from other mice, and she is dissatisfied with her lot, although she doesn't quite know why. A captive dove tells her of the woods and fields and how it feels to fly, for she is a house mouse and knows nothing of the world outside. In her compassion for her friend, the mousewife sets the dove free:

> He did not see her or look towards her; then – clap – he took her breath away so that she fell. He had opened his wings and flown straight out. For a moment he dipped as if he would fall, his wings were cramped, and then he moved them and lifted up and up and flew away across the tops of the trees.
> The mousewife picked herself up and shook out her bones and fur.
> 'So that is to fly,' she said . . . 'Now there is no one to tell me about the hills and the corn and the clouds . . .'

For me this story has all the compassion, integrity and skilled economy of words so characteristic of Rumer Godden.

Eleanor Farjeon's 'Elsie Piddock Skips in her Sleep' was written in her Sussex cottage as children skipped in the lane outside. It was her favourite story amongst the many she wrote, for she felt that it said what she wanted to say more than any others. It is the story of Elsie Piddock, who, when she was a child, skipped with the fairies and who, when she was 109 years old, saved Mount Caburn for the children of Glynde and for the fairies by her magical skipping. She is still skipping and:

> . . . If you go to Caburn at the new moon, you may catch a glimpse of a tiny bent figure, no bigger than a child, skipping all by itself in its sleep, and hear a gay little voice, like the voice of a dancing yellow leaf, singing:
> '*An*dy *span*dy *sugar*dy *can*dy, *French al*mond *rock*!
> Breadandbutterforyoursupper'sallyourmother'sgot!'

I **cannot tell** this story without remembering the lively, affectionate person who was Eleanor Farjeon.

Telling stories like these is more difficult than telling a folk tale, but it is infinitely worthwhile for both storyteller and audience. It demands not only experience but empathy with the author. I have had the good fortune to know both Rumer Godden and Eleanor Farjeon as friends for many years, but it is not necessary, of course, to know an author personally in order to capture the essence of a story. To alter the wording of stories of this calibre would be impertinent. A little abridging may be legitimate, but that is all.

The best stories deserve telling more than once. We may want to repeat them many times, sometimes with long intervals between each telling. One way to remind yourself of them quickly is to keep a story notebook in which you enter the outlines of stories that have proved worthy of telling again. (A few entries from my own story notebooks are included at the end of this chapter.) It may be as detailed as you have time for – the more detailed it is, the easier it will be to recover the story from your memory. It is also useful to compile a subject index so that you can find suitable stories for a particular occasion.

The process of memorizing a story means very much more than just reading it through a short while before you are to tell it. In order to tell a story effectively the storyteller must

- see it in her imagination;
- hear what the characters are saying, feel what they are feeling;
- be prepared to spend time and energy on learning it.

Practice and experience enable the storyteller to bring out the full potential of a story. Once it is absorbed in this way, it becomes a personal experience and a new creation every time you tell it. The very fact that it has not been learnt word for word, but has become part of you, means that there is no necessity to use the same words every time. The storyteller is free, and so is the story.

Entries from
Eileen Colwell's Story Notebooks

The Three Sillies
from *English Fairy Tales* by Joseph Jacobs

PART ONE

Opening sentence
'Once upon a time there was a farmer and his wife who had one daughter, and she was courted by a gentleman.'

Gentleman visits farm each evening, girl goes down to cellar to draw beer for him. One evening she notices an axe sticking in the beam over her head.

Quote 'Supposing him and me was to be married and we was to have a son and he was to come down into the cellar to draw beer like as I'm doing now, and that there axe was to fall on his head and kill him, what a dreadful thing it would be!'

Sits down to cry.

a) Mother comes down – beer running over the floor.
Asks daughter what is the matter. *Repeat quote*

b) Father comes down – beer running all over the floor.
Asks mother what is the matter. *Repeat quote*
Father sits down to cry.

c) Gentleman comes down. Sees beer all over the floor.
Turns off tap of barrel. Asks father what is the matter. *Repeat quote*

Gentleman laughs, pulls out axe from beam, says: 'I've never met three such big sillies as you three before. When I can find three bigger sillies than you three, then I'll come back and marry your daughter.'

PART TWO

Gentleman sets out on travels. Comes to
a) Cottage where woman is trying to persuade cow to

climb ladder to roof (where grass is growing). Tells her to climb ladder herself and throw grass down. She drives cow up ladder, ties rope round it, drops end down chimney and ties it round her waist. Cow falls, woman jerked up chimney. ONE BIG SILLY.

   b) Man at inn gets up early each morning, fastens trousers to knobs of chest-of-drawers, runs and tries to jump into them. Gentleman suggests proper way to put on trousers. TWO BIG SILLIES.

   c) Villagers trying to rescue moon from pond with rakes, brooms, pitchforks. Gentleman tells them it is only *reflection* of moon in pond. Villagers chase him away. THREE BIG SILLIES.

Concluding sentence
'So the gentleman turned back home again and married the farmer's daughter, and if they didn't live happily for ever after, that's nothing to do with you or me.'

The Dog That Had No Name
by Leila Berg
[Example of a simple story for very young children]

Opening sentence
'Once upon a time there was a dog. He was a very jolly dog . . . [the description can be as the storyteller pleases, or as a child requests]. But he had no name at all. "I shall go and find a name," he said, and off he ran . . . '

He meets –
1. Man mending the road. [Each person met says, 'Hello, little dog.'] Name suggested: PAT.
2. Lady shopping. BESS.
3. Window cleaner. GYP.
4. Postman. ROUGH. Dog despairs of ever finding a name.
5. Children. TRIX. 'I bet Trix is my name!'

'And the children and the little dog ran off together. The children laughed and shouted, the little dog barked, for they were going home and the little dog had found his name.'

N.B. A few 'wuffs' by the little dog are appreciated, but don't allow *too* prolonged, enthusiastic audience participation!

Two of Everything: A Chinese Story
from *The Treasure of Li-Po* by Alice Ritchie

Introduction. Mr and Mrs Hak-tak were rather old and rather poor. All they had was a mud hut and a tiny patch of land on which they grew the vegetables which were their only food. When it was a good season, Mr Hak-tak sold a few vegetables in the next village so that he could buy seed, oil for the lamp and very occasionally a length of cotton stuff to make himself or his wife a new coat or trousers.

How it began. Mr Hak-tak finds in his plot a large brass jar. Decides to take it home – puts his purse inside it for safety. Staggers into house.

Mrs Hak-tak asks its use. Mr Hak-tak says, 'It is too large for a cooking-pot, too small for a bath. So far it has been useful for carrying home my purse.'

Mrs Hak-tak looks into pot. In so doing she drops her one hairpin (carved bone). Puts in her hand to get it out again.

The discovery. Pulls out original purse and hairpin and finds there is –
    a. still a purse and hairpin there (exactly the same).
    b. 'Let us put in the sack of lentils.'
Two sacks of lentils.
    c. Blanket. Two blankets (both threadbare).
    d. Wadded coat. Two wadded coats (both shabby).
    e. Mrs Hak-tak (a woman of great intelligence) suggests

putting in purse again and again so that there will be money to buy *new* clothes, etc. Floor soon covered with old purses.

f. They put in money only, until there is a great deal of money. Tie it up in blanket and go to bed.

Further developments. Mr Hak-tak goes to market to buy what they want. Mrs Hak-tak tidies up, gets dinner cooking, makes herself a set of hairpins and a few other oddments with help of jar. Sleeps. Tries a cabbage leaf in pot to make sure it is working properly. 'I do not know how you came to us, my dear pot, but you are the best friend we ever had.'

The disaster. Mrs Hak-tak leans over the pot, hears her husband returning, turns round and OVERBALANCES.

Mr Hak-tak pulls her out. Another pair of legs kicks in the jar. He pulls out another Mrs Hak-tak. The first Mrs Hak-tak shouts 'I will not have a second Mrs Hak-tak in the house.' Weeps. Blames her husband for pulling out second Mrs Hak-tak. Tells him to put her back again. 'What, and draw out two more!' Mr Hak-tak steps back and OVERBALANCES.

Two Mrs Hak-taks pull him out. Another pair of legs. Another Mr Hak-tak. Both exactly alike.

Solution. Mrs Hak-tak proposes that new Mr and Mrs Hak-tak shall live together in a new house, which they will build next door.

This they do. Live together in great friendliness. Mrs Hak-tak says second Mrs Hak-tak is more than a sister to her. Mr Hak-tak says the same of second Mr Hak-tak.

Conclusion. 'So they lived happily together and never lacked for money again. But when anybody was in trouble, Mr and Mrs Hak-tak always helped them, for had they not the jar which would give them two of everything?'

The Magic Umbrella
adapted by Eileen Colwell from Rose Fyleman's story
[An example of a story that has found its present form over many years of storytelling and audience participation]

Opening sentence

'Once upon a time there was a wizard who had a magic umbrella. One night he went to a meeting of witches and wizards in [market the audience knows] market place and forgot his umbrella. An old farmer found it leaning against a stall and, as no one claimed it, he took it home to his wife . . . '

– A MAGIC UMBRELLA: If you held it open and counted THREE, you found yourself at home . . .

– If you counted FIVE, you found yourself where you most wished to be . . .

– If you counted SEVEN, you found yourself at the top of the nearest church steeple . . .

1. Farmer's wife to market on a wet day. Counts out THREE eggs and finds herself at home in her own kitchen. Daughter's astonishment.
2. Visits married daughter, sits by busy road holding umbrella as shade. Interested in cars – 'I wish I was in one of them . . .' Counts to FIVE.
3. Goes to doctor because of queer happenings. Counts pills (SEVEN) and finds herself flying round steeple with umbrella as parachute.

Conclusion. Daughter fetches firemen who tow her down by her skirts. Umbrella blows away – old woman never ill again in that way.

Final sentence

'BUT – if you should find an umbrella which doesn't belong to you, be careful. You don't want to find yourself floating round the church steeple. Do you!'

N.B. Characterization obvious. Suggest by small details. Farmer's wife a simple soul, much bewildered by what is happening to her. Her daughter is not very bright. Suggest a dialect, one that is natural to you. Pause when you have counted SEVEN and then look upward to the imaginary church steeple – every child will know what has happened.

This ending was not in the original story. I have added it at the children's demand because they wanted to know 'what happened next'.

BOOKS & STORIES MENTIONED

Hans C. Andersen, 'The Nightingale', in Lisbeth Zwerger's picture book, Neugebauer, and in Erik Haugaard's *Hans Andersen – His Classic Fairy Tales*, Gollancz

Leila Berg, 'The Dog That Had No Name', in Eileen Colwell's *Time for a Story*, Young Puffin

Elizabeth Clark, 'The Tale of a Turnip', in Eileen Colwell's *Tell Me a Story*, Young Puffin

Walter de la Mare, *Tales Told Again*, Faber, o.p.

Eleanor Farjeon, 'Elsie Piddock Skips in Her Sleep', in *Martin Pippin in the Daisy Field*, Oxford University Press, o.p.

Rose Fyleman, 'The Magic Umbrella', in Sara & Stephen Corrin's *More Stories for Under-Fives*, Young Puffin

Wanda Gág, *Gone is Gone*, in Virginia Haviland's *The Fairy Tale Treasury*, Hamish Hamilton / Picture Puffin

Wanda Gág, *Millions of Cats*, Faber / Puffin

Rumer Godden, 'The Mousewife', in *Mouse Time*, Magnet

Laurence Housman, 'A Chinese Fairy Tale', in *Stories for Eight-Year-Olds* ed. Sara & Stephen Corrin, Faber / Puffin

Joseph Jacobs, 'The Three Sillies', in *English Fairy Tales*, Dover; in Sara & Stephen Corrin's *Stories for Seven-Year-Olds*, Faber/Puffin; and in Paul Galdone's picture book, Heinemann

Rudyard Kipling, 'The Elephant's Child', in Sara & Stephen Corrin's *Stories for Seven-Year-Olds*, Faber / Puffin

Rudyard Kipling, *Just So Stories*, Macmillan or Viking Kestrel

Sir Thomas Malory, *Morte D'Arthur*, Dent

Alice Ritchie, 'Two of Everything', in *More Stories for Under-Fives* ed. Sara & Stephen Corrin, Young Puffin

'Tom Tit Tot', in Joseph Jacobs's *English Fairy Tales*, Dover, and in Alan Garner's *Book of British Fairy Tales*, Collins

Oscar Wilde, 'The Selfish Giant', in *The Fairy Stories of Oscar Wilde*, Gollancz; in Oscar Wilde's *Stories for Children*, Simon & Schuster; and in Lisbeth Zwerger's picture book, Neugebauer

7

Improving Your Voice and Speech

After the adaptation of the story itself, there comes the actual telling, and here *voice* – the way you produce your voice, that is – and *diction*, the degree of clarity with which you speak – are all-important. As with making a speech, it is not only what is said but *how* it is said that makes storytelling a success or failure. Some knowledge of and skill in 'how to get it over' are essential. The storyteller needs to know how to use her voice, for this is the instrument on which much of the story's impact depends. It is the storyteller's responsibility to make sure her voice is audible. If children have to strain to hear what you are saying, they will soon lose interest.

A pleasantly modulated voice is a gift, but much can be done to improve any voice, especially when there are particular difficulties. Most voices need strengthening. Even when speaking to small groups it is not enough to use a conversational tone; the voice must be 'enlarged'. Actors can, by using their voices correctly, be heard distinctly in every part of the theatre, and the storyteller must learn this skill.

The quickest way to learn how to use the voice correctly, of course, is to have a few lessons in voice production. Information about private teachers of speech can be found in the local press, or there may be an evening class at a local centre. Particulars of such classes are usually available in libraries. For myself I found that three terms with a private teacher who concentrated on teaching me how to use my voice and how to breathe correctly – and who enjoyed listening to stories and did not try to teach me an 'elocutionary' style – was an excellent investment. As a result I have never suffered from a strained throat – but if such lessons are impossible, here are a few hints that may be helpful.

Easy and correct breathing, properly controlled, is the foundation of good speaking. Most people breathe shallowly from the top of the chest. This results in tightness, and any attempt to increase volume causes strain. Practise breathing from the diaphragm, feeling the expansion of the lower ribs with your hands as you breathe and filling the lungs to capacity. This will help to develop a good clear tone. Humming is a useful exercise, using the vowel sounds, first with the letter M before them and then with B. This helps to improve nasal resonance, which produces a musical quality in the voice.

Every member of your audience must be able to hear you; however, this does not mean that you need to shout or use a 'booming' voice. Indeed, this often distorts and confuses the sound of words. Beware of talking to yourself or telling the story to the front row only. Direct your voice to the back of the room and lift your head so that you can see everyone there. Think of your breath as coming from directly in front of your face rather than from your throat and you will find that gradually you will be able to 'throw' your voice so that it carries to the back of the room. This is not forcing the voice – to do so would result in a strained throat – but is a gentle and gradual process helped by thinking carefully about what you are trying to do.

A knowledge of how to control your breathing so that you make the best possible use of your voice helps to give confidence in telling a story. If you are concerned that the audience cannot hear you or worried that your voice may fail, this will very likely lead to a feeling of tension that will not only affect you but the story and the audience as well. Clear speaking and pronunciation are essential so that storytelling becomes a pleasure for everyone concerned.

Clear diction is also essential. Slurred or clipped words,

slipshod speech, make it difficult for those listening. As an exercise, try saying nursery rhymes aloud, slowly at first and then at varying speeds. Tongue-twisters, jingles and nonsense verses like Lewis Carroll's 'Lobster Quadrille' or 'Jabberwocky' will all help in the mastery of clear speech, for they must be carefully spoken. Be wary, however, not to develop the habit of exaggerated 'mouthing' of the words as some singers do. Overdone pronunciation is unpleasant to watch and to hear. You should aim to develop a natural way of speech that is both clear and pleasant.

A common fault is dropping the voice at the end of a sentence. This 'falling inflection' makes for a sing-song delivery – a sure way to send the audience to sleep. It may also mean that children miss a vital word that is necessary for the understanding of the story. For example: 'Once upon a time there was a man and his wife who had but one son and he was blind . . . ' Drop your voice on that vital word 'blind' and many children will not hear it and will lose the key to the story.

Have you ever listened to your voice on a tape recorder? It will be a salutary experience, revealing unrealized faults and any wrong use of the voice. Note whether you have a tendency to speak monotonously or in a minor key – this can sound depressing – or to stumble over words or to fill a pause with 'er'. All these drawbacks can be overcome once you are conscious of them.

Everyone must have suffered from having to listen to the public speaker who delivers his whole speech at the same level of voice and pace. Very soon the message, however well prepared and significant, ceases to have any meaning for those listening. Constant variety in pace and pitch is vital if your audience is to remain alert and responsive.

Obviously, pace and tone depend upon the kind of story you are telling. Compare a story like Andersen's gently satirical 'The Nightingale' with the vigorous, down-to-earth folk tale 'Molly Whuppie', and it will be obvious that the two differ as much in pace as they do in mood.

It is as well to start any story fairly slowly to give the audience time to become used to your voice and personality.

68

To hurry unduly through nervousness means that some children are unable to follow the story; to tell a story too slowly is tedious and uninteresting for the listener. A judicious blend of variety in pace and tone makes a story more stimulating and easier to listen to. The human voice has infinite potential for expressing mood and character. Youth and age, timidity and courage, king and peasant can all be suggested by the tone and pitch of the voice as well as by small mannerisms and choice of words.

In spite of all your preparation, you will almost certainly feel a little nervous before telling a story. This happens to the most experienced storytellers and, oddly enough, is an advantage, for a little nervousness tends to heighten your sensibility and awareness. Taking a deep breath will help. Look round your audience in a friendly way – it isn't their fault if you are feeling inadequate and fearful! The important thing is to make this first attempt; the second is never as difficult.

BOOKS & STORIES MENTIONED

Hans C. Andersen, *The Nightingale*, in Lisbeth Zwerger's picture book, Neugebauer, and in Erik Haugaard's *Hans Andersen – His Classic Fairy Tales*, Gollancz

Lewis Carroll, 'The Lobster Quadrille' in *Alice's Adventures in Wonderland* and 'Jabberwocky' in *Through the Looking-Glass*, Macmillan

'Molly Whuppie', Errol Le Cain's picture book, Faber / Puffin; in Alan Garner's *Book of British Fairy Tales*, Collins; in Kathleen Lines's *The Faber Storybook*, Faber; and in James Reeves's *English Fables and Fairy Stories*, Oxford University Press

8

Facing the Audience

Whatever the occasion or venue, the practical question of accommodation must always be the storyteller's first consideration for a storytelling session. There are two physical essentials for storytelling – a quiet place, free from interruption, and comfortable conditions for both teller and audience. Seldom is the storyteller blessed in this way, and she must always be ready to adjust to circumstances, however unfavourable. Sometimes the only suitable place to tell a story is in the corner of a busy room with, at most, a screen of some kind to give the illusion of privacy.

In an open-plan school or library a quiet spot may be hard to find, and in a playgroup environment, where there may be only one large room for all activities, it can be even harder. In one Book Week session I was allotted a 'quiet corner' through which waves of noisy children, engaged in more vigorous pursuits, swept in and out yelling so fiercely that the younger children in my audience clustered round me for reassurance. Another problem can be caused by curious adults who, having disturbed the children's concentration, drift away again. Polite firmness is the only answer to such interruptions.

As for comfortable conditions for the audience, it is unreasonable to expect children to sit on the floor for any length of time without fidgeting. Fidgeting is infectious and disturbs both audience and storyteller. If children have to sit in a cramped position, make an interval between stories for them to stretch their arms at least – or, if it is possible, to stand up and turn round three times. Cushions are a help but are apt to be appropriated by the strongest or used as weapons. Gaily coloured stools are much enjoyed by little children and are guarded jealously – they may be used as trains if the children are unsupervised. Some modern libraries have tiered steps where children can sit quite comfortably. Avoid the formality of rows, for serried ranks of children can give a feeling of faceless anonymity. A semi-circle of seats is always preferable to straight rows, as long as it does not cover too wide an area. A gangway down the centre of the room makes it difficult for the storyteller to 'gather the eyes' of the audience. To be compelled to turn one's head from side to side like a demented weathercock in order to see the audience is tiring for the storyteller and unrestful for everyone else.

It would be reassuring to expect that an audience can always be restricted to a small number, ideally about twenty, but this is rarely the case. The storyteller must be prepared to tackle any number, according to circumstances. As a visiting storyteller to schools, I meet audiences varying from fifty to as many as three hundred, which is certainly not a desirable number. If at all possible, fifty is the maximum for intimate storytelling. Any greater number needs a storyteller of considerable experience and confidence, or the occasion may get out of hand and become too impersonal.

Some storytellers like to sit in a comfortable chair when telling a story to suggest informality. Others stand – as I do myself – in order to see the audience more easily and to be free to move a little. Never sit or stand behind a table or lectern, for this creates a barrier between audience and storyteller. It is important to be able to see *all* the children and for them to see the storyteller. A faceless voice is much more difficult to listen to because there is no focus for the eyes and the attention. The storyteller should always try to sit or stand naturally, without fidgeting with anything, which may distract the children's attention from the story. Storytelling should be restful to watch as well as to hear.

These practical details may seem unimportant, but to neglect them is to risk disappointment when the story is told. An apparent informality is often a tribute to careful plan-ning, which allows a relaxed approach to the actual telling of the story.

71

And so the moment comes to face the audience. This is the test of all the selection and preparation that has gone before. The storyteller has no props, no costume, no scenery, only the story to share with the children. A live audience can be a terrifying experience, and it is natural to feel nervous. It is the story that matters, however, and remembering this will help to banish self-consciousness.

First, show the children the book the story comes from, if there is one. It is important to establish firmly in children's minds the fact that books are a rich source of stories. It is prudent to introduce the story by some general phrase like 'This is a story about finding treasure . . .' or 'This story is about a prince who had three wishes . . .' rather than by its title. If the title is familiar, some child will state uncompromisingly 'I've heard *that* story!' implying that he never wants to hear it again. This can be disconcerting to a storyteller who has painstakingly prepared one particular story and no other.

Preface the story by a brief explanation of anything that might puzzle children, for it is easy to assume that the audience is as knowledgeable as you are. While children should be stimulated to use their imagination and can easily *see* such fantastic creatures as fairies, giants or fabulous monsters, they cannot be expected to form an accurate mental picture of a real animal they have never encountered. So before telling a story from a book like Grey Owl's *The Adventures of Sajo and Her Beaver People*, it would be a good idea to show the children pictures of beavers and a lodge. Princes and princesses can be imagined much more romantically by children than by adults, but if the story is about a real person or place, some visual aid is needed.

No one can tell you exactly how to tell a story, for that is an individual matter which changes according to the individual personalities of different storytellers. Each person has a natural way of expressing what she wants to say, and copying someone else makes for insincerity. There are certain pitfalls and difficulties, however, for which the storyteller should be prepared.

Avoid rhetorical questions with children of all ages, but

particularly with young children. Very naturally children think that if someone asks a question, she wants an answer! 'He looked into the garden and what do you think he saw?' asks a storyteller in a playgroup. 'An elephant,' a boy answers confidently. 'No dear,' says the storyteller kindly, 'it was only a *small* garden.' 'It was a small elephant,' says the child firmly. The story is ruined, for the kitten the storyteller meant to introduce is now an anti-climax. Every storyteller has had an experience like this.

And the interruptions! We are all familiar with the young child who says in the middle of a story, 'Look at my new shoes!' or 'Sometimes I wear yellow trousers . . . ' A story about a dog can elicit the comment 'Our dog has a fur coat right down to his knees . . . ' Theoretically such interruptions should be woven into the story, but this is not always humanly possible. One thing is certain with an audience of young children – such comments cannot be ignored, for the child will persist until she receives some attention. What form this acknowledgement takes depends on the kind of interruption. It is usually completely irrelevant, in which case you can only say 'Yes, Mary!' or 'Tell me about it afterwards' or 'What fun!' and carry on with the story *immediately*. Usually the child is satisfied once she has been noticed. With older children, however, it is usually possible to establish a tradition that the story should not be interrupted because it breaks the continuity for the others. Occasionally this rule is broken catastrophically. On one occasion when I was telling the story of 'Lazy Tok' I said, quoting from the book, ' "Shen mao tung shi!" – that's Chinese . . . ' 'No, it isn't,' came a voice from the audience, a Chinese boy from Hong Kong. I lost face, decidedly.

When showing a picture book to young children it is essential that all of them can see it easily; otherwise their cries of 'Can't see!' 'Show *me*!' can turn into quite violent protests. Allow time for the picture to be absorbed and comments made: 'I don't like that picture, I can't tell what it is.' 'My auntie wears a yellow jumper like that . . . '

Sometimes participation is welcome and differs from interruption in that it implies absorption rather than inattention and involves the audience in the story. Little children love making train or animal noises, but take care that this doesn't get out of hand, especially if the animal in question is a pig! Older children enjoy an occasional chant or nonsense rhyme in which they can participate. 'Did you feed my cow?', 'I went to the animal fair', or 'What did you put in your pocket?' can all give shared pleasure.

Gesture can be a problem. How much should the storyteller use? If you are really *in* the story, gesture and facial expression will come naturally, just as they do in conversation, and will arise spontaneously from the story itself. For example, length, height and direction call for a simple explanatory gesture. Beware of exaggerated movements, however, for they can easily look ludicrous. I shall never forget a visiting storyteller who recited Walter de la Mare's 'Off the Ground':

> Three Jolly Farmers
> Once bet a pound
> Each dance the others would
> Off the ground . . .

She acted every movement suggested in the poem and became so exhausted that I had to help her from the platform. Her extravagant actions at first excited the children to laughter, then to obvious boredom. Storytelling, if made too dramatic, becomes a performance, for overdramatization centres attention on the storyteller rather than the story.

Dialect – and by dialect I mean any kind of colloquial speech, unfamiliar idioms, odd or ungrammatical speech – is often a difficulty, for some stories can lose their impact if told without it. Consider the Brer Rabbit stories. Imagine such a sentence as 'Brer Fox, he wink his eye slow, en lay low, en de Tar-Baby she ain't sayin' nuthin'', translated into everyday grammatical speech. What it would lose! A tale like 'Tom Tit Tot' seems colourless in standard English compared with the Suffolk dialect: 'That were grinning from ear to ear, an lawk! how that twirled that's tail!' If it seems impossible to imitate the intonation and distinctive vowel sounds of a dialect, it is

better to leave such stories alone rather than use a phoney accent.

In many stories, however, it is sufficient to suggest the part of the country from which a story comes by a turn of phrase or a local word. 'Thee do movey, do'ee,' says the woodcutter in Somerset as he chops the dragon in half. 'Only mortal this dragon is, 'tis brave you are!' exclaims a lad in a Welsh tale. 'EE-ee!' says a man from Lancashire. 'You're nobbut a child!' 'Yon's a wee tyke!' remarks someone from Northumberland. But always remember that too much dialect can puzzle a child from another country – or even county.

As you begin telling the story you will realize that the time spent deciding upon the opening sentence was not wasted; the fact that you know it so well will help to overcome your nervousness. Suddenly the story gathers momentum and takes over from the storyteller. You should be there *in* the story, able to see the characters and take part in their adventures. As you near the climax of the story, there comes 'a catch of the breath, a beat and lifting of the heart' as Tolkien describes it.

This intense involvement is helped by the use of what actors call the dramatic pause, a slowing down and pause just before the climax. Your audience will hang breathlessly on such a pause, and even if some children have already guessed what is going to happen next, it will enable other, perhaps slower, children to realize it too. A good example is found in 'Where Arthur Sleeps', in which a thief has to edge round a great bronze bell for, if he rings it, Arthur's knights will wake up. Inch by inch he edges round it . . . inch . . . by . . . inch. What will happen? A similar tension is found in 'Fierce Feathers', when into the silent Quaker meeting house come fourteen redskins in full war paint with poisoned arrows held taut to bow strings . . .

After the climax of the story the ending should follow quickly. The immediate reaction to a story can be unexpected. On one occasion when I had just told an exciting story, there was a moment of silence and then a boy leapt to his feet and cried, 'Three cheers! Hip-hip-hip . . .!' and the whole company of two hundred children joined in a deafening cheer. This was quite unpremeditated, a spontaneous release from the tension of an exciting story.

The greatest tribute that can be paid to a story is the moment of silence that sometimes follows. Such a moment of emotion and delight, the recognition of a perfect story, can come after stories of the calibre of Laurence Housman's 'A Chinese Fairy Tale' or Eleanor Farjeon's 'Elsie Piddock Skips in her Sleep'. The child has been lost in another world, and it takes a little time to return to the everyday. Let him have that interlude. Don't spoil his pleasure and the impression left on heart and mind by letting the mundane intrude too soon. To tell your audience immediately and abruptly 'Time to go home! Put away your chairs and go out quietly' is to destroy something irrecoverable.

But after most stories there can be as many comments and questions as time allows. 'Are there any dinosaurs now?' asks one little girl. 'No, silly, they've all gone to heaven!' replies another child piously. 'That was a heart-rending story,' says an older girl sniffing surreptitiously. 'Now I call Long John Silver a *proper* pirate!' comments a boy, drawing a finger across his throat. 'Don't you worry about that dragon,' say two little boys wearing firemen's helmets and carrying rubber axes. 'We'll chop it up for you!' And after a story to introduce Erich Kästner's *Emil and the Detectives*, a boy says, 'If Emil's mother had sent the money by postal order instead of giving it to Emil to take by train, there wouldn't have been all that trouble.' (Nor all that story, either!) The storyteller should always be ready to listen to comments made by children, not only out of natural friendly interest but because such observations are helpful in judging the impact of the story.

If the story has really become part of you, you will find that something else has happened: you are able to tell it while at the same time watching the reaction of the audience. Is the story too long? Does its humour really appeal to children? Perhaps a certain passage that seemed particularly good in preparation is not, in fact, so effective, for the children look puzzled. Has the fate of the wicked stepmother or the sudden appearance of a ghostly creature frightened some children? If so, it must be toned down next time. Perhaps, on the other hand, the story has been made too tame for children for the sake of satisfying adult sensibilities? You can learn a great deal about the story – and yourself – by watching critically how it is received.

A word of warning. A storyteller should realize that she has power which must never be used for its own sake. To tell stories of the trivial kind, which depend for their impact on sensationalism or crude humour, or to present a story with exaggerated gestures in order to excite easy laughter, is to reduce storytelling to the lowest level of entertainment. This is 'playing to the gallery', which may well gain applause for the storyteller and provide a superficial and transitory pleasure for the audience, but it is a sad misuse of the power that Story gives us, and is not the purpose of storytelling.

Sincerity and integrity are essential in any relationship with children. It is our privilege to be the medium through which children hear stories that give them lasting enjoyment, stories of adventure and danger, stories that amuse, stories whose beauty and compassion make them an emotional experience and touch the hearts of both storyteller and child.

In Haiti, when a storyteller feels he has a story to tell, he says to the audience 'Cric?' If he is approved, the people respond 'Crac!' and he can tell his story. If not, he must yield his place to another storyteller.
    May your 'Cric?' always be answered by 'Crac!'

BOOKS & STORIES MENTIONED

'Brer Rabbit', in Julius Lester's *The Tales of Uncle Remus: The Adventures of Brer Rabbit*, Bodley Head / Pan

'Did you feed my cow?', title poem in collection by Margaret Taylor, T.Y. Crowell, o.p.

Eleanor Farjeon, 'Elsie Piddock Skips in Her Sleep', in *Martin Pippin in the Daisy Field*, Oxford University Press, o.p.

'Fierce Feathers' by L.V. Hodgkin, *The Magic Umbrella* ed. Eileen Colwell, Bodley Head, o.p.

Laurence Housman, 'A Chinese Fairy Tale', in Sara & Stephen Corrin's *Stories for Eight-Year-Olds*, Faber / Puffin

'I went to the animal fair', in *The Song That Sings the Bird* ed. Ruth Craft, Collins

Erich Kästner, *Emil and the Detectives*, Cape / Puffin

'Lazy Tok', by Mervyn Skipper, in Judith Elkin's *The New Golden Land Anthology*, Viking Kestrel / Puffin

Grey Owl, *The Adventures of Sajo and Her Beaver People*, Heinemann Educ., o.p.

'Tom Tit Tot', by Joseph Jacobs in his *English Fairy Tales*, Dover, and in Alan Garner's *Book of British Fairy Tales*, Collins

'What did you put in your pocket?', by Beatrice Schenk de Regniers, in Judith Elkin's *The New Golden Land Anthology*, Viking Kestrel / Puffin

'Where Arthur Sleeps', in Gwyn Jones's *Welsh Legends and Folk-tales*, Puffin, and in Judith Elkin's *The New Golden Land Anthology*, Viking Kestrel / Puffin

9

Special Situations

All kinds of activities centre on books each year, organized by libraries and schools, publishers, Book Trust, and the Federation of Children's Book Groups. They appear under many names from 'Book Fairs' to 'Book Weeks' to 'Book Bangs', and storytelling takes place during most of them. The Federation sponsors an annual 'National Tell a Story Week', during which the emphasis is on storytelling in the many groups up and down the country.

Hallowe'en and Christmas are two occasions that offer excellent occasions for storytelling.

Hallowe'en, traditionally the evening when ghosts and demons roam the land, is obviously the time for stories about witches and ghosts. Such stories are doubly effective when told by the light of a candle in a turnip lantern. (Melons are easier to carve but, when overheated, their smell is appalling!) It is also worth decorating the room with a background of witches, broomsticks and black cats to create a suitable atmosphere. Stories can be found in Ruth Manning-Sanders's *A Book of Witches* and *A Book of Sorcerers and Spells* and in my own *Hallowe'en Acorn*. Eerie poems can add atmosphere: try e. e. cummings's 'hist whist', with its shattering closing 'WheeE E E!'. Barbara Ireson's anthology of witchy poems called *Shadows and Spells* is very useful for such occasions.

Ghost stories are also very popular with children. The pleasure in these tales is compounded of a love of the mysterious and the unexplained – a ghost tale that is rationalized is not worth telling – and an element of fear about what may happen. Obviously stories of this kind must be told with caution, or indignant parents may descend upon the storyteller. As long as the atmosphere is festive and not too serious, and there are adults around to give a feeling of security, ghost stories are innocuous. There are many collections available, from Ruth Manning-Sanders's *A Book of Ghosts and Goblins* to the much more subtle and chilling *The Shadow-Cage and Other Tales of the Supernatural* by Philippa Pearce.

Children half believe these stories. I remember telling a ridiculous tale called 'The Water Ghost' to a group of children. In it a ghost appeared annually, dripping water over the carpets of a stately home. It was finally 'laid' by the twentieth-century heir: he had it frozen and placed in cold storage. After the story was over, several children asked me quite seriously for the telephone number of the cold storage firm so that they could ring up and ask whether the water ghost was still immobilized.

For older children, Dickens's 'The Signalman' is notable for its eeriness and feeling of doom:

> I . . . ran towards the figure, calling 'What's wrong? What has happened?' It stood just outside the entrance to the tunnel. I advanced so close to it that I wondered at its keeping the sleeve across its eyes. I ran right up to it and had my hand stretched out to pull the sleeve away – there was no one there.

A very unusual ghost story is Joan Aiken's 'Humble-puppy'. The narrator hears a sound and looks inside a deed box bought at an auction. Nothing there. The noise persists, and as she puts her hand into the box again she feels 'a small, bony, warm, trembling body with big awkward feet, and silky dangling ears, and a cold nose . . . ' It is a ghost puppy! Or what about this for an encore, surely the most laconic ghost story in existence, a West Country folk tale:

> There were two fellows out working in a field, hoeing turnips they was, and the one he stop and lean on his hoe and he mop his face and he say, 'Yur – I don't believe in

these yer ghostesses!'
And t'other man say, 'Don't 'ee?'
AND HE VANISHED.

Christmas is another children's festival when stories are welcome, set against the background of a Christmas tree. Many Christmas stories are hidden away in collections of folk tales, and it is worth keeping a note of any that appeal to you when you come across them. Ruth Sawyer's 'Schnitzle, Schnotzle and Schnootzle' is a good story, and Elizabeth Clark has a number in her various collections, notably 'Brother Johannick and his Silver Bell', a legend from Brittany. Children often enjoy hearing the same story again and again. In my own library it became a tradition to tell Ursula Moray Williams's 'The Good Little Christmas Tree' every year. A little tree, in its compassion for two children whose parents cannot afford the usual ornaments, buys pretty things for that purpose, paying for them with its own needles so that it becomes bare and ugly. The refrain is cumulative, always ending with the phrase 'and the cookies bobbing about like little brown mice', which children love to share. Many beautiful poems have been written about Christmas – look for them in such collections as James Reeves's *The Christmas Book*, an anthology of stories, poems and carols, and the Corrins' *Puffin Book of Christmas Stories*.

Diwali is also a lovely festival to celebrate by storytelling. There are many stories and customs that can be incorporated into a story session – if you are lucky, there will be a child in the group who not only knows the festival and the significance of certain colours and patterns but may even have patterns painted on her hands.

One international festival that should not be forgotten is Children's Book Day, inaugurated by the International Board on Books for Young People to commemorate Hans Christian Andersen's birthday, 2 April. This is obviously an occasion for children to hear some of Andersen's stories and something about his life which, in some aspects, is itself so like a fairy tale. It is an opportunity to remind children of 'The Ugly Duckling' (the real story – not the film version!),

'The Snow Queen' and 'The Emperor's New Clothes', stories no child should miss. Each year a different nation sponsors a poster by a national artist for the anniversary, and this is available in every country.

There are particular people in the community who *need* stories – children in hospital, in long-term care, or being home-educated. In hospitals long-term patients are often bored and lack mental stimulation, so that the arrival of a visitor, particularly with a story, is always welcome. An appropriate time must be arranged with the hospital staff, of course, so that the storyteller does not interfere with hospital routine. The length and type of stories will depend on the physical state of the patient.

I would make a special plea for storytelling to the visually impaired, a group of which I have some experience. These children are lively, demonstrative and enjoy participation. Their reaction to a story is just as quick as that of a sighted child. There are difficulties, for it has to be remembered that details of the story usually conveyed by actions or facial expressions must be translated into sounds and words. I have found, however, that my greatest fear – that these children might not be able to form a mental picture of things that they had never seen and that are taken for granted by sighted children – was unfounded. I do not know what they 'see' when I speak of fields, flowers, the sky, for they rely so much on touch and sound, but undoubtedly it is something that satisfies them. As the story progresses, they clap their hands with excitement, jump up and ask, 'Did he get away? Is it going to be all right?' If I pause unduly, there will be anxious inquiries, 'Are you still there?' They need constant physical touch – I can still feel their fluttering fingers trace the outline of my face, and I will never forget one child's meditative comment as she did so – 'I should think she's sixteen,' a supposition which was, alas, very far from the truth.

Children with hearing loss are a little more difficult for most storytellers as the children depend not on sound but on lipreading and signed interpretation of the story. These children appreciate more expansive gestures, which help them understand what is being said. It is obviously ideal if the teller is able to sign (only forty per cent of conversation can be lipread); if this isn't possible, there is usually a teacher or parent who can interpret for the child.

With physically handicapped children you can tell stories as you would to any child. In my audience I have had children with muscular dystrophy and others so seriously disabled that half my listeners were in wheelchairs. Rather than selecting a 'special' story, I chose one about children able to do adventurous things. A thalidomide child of three identified herself with the child I named after her in my story – for a brief space she *was* that other child, with the use of all her limbs, and she beamed with delight.

Emotionally disturbed children are another matter. A story can help a distressed child, but there is always a danger that, if the storyteller is ignorant of the particular problem, the story may be very upsetting – a scary story, for instance, or a deeply emotional one such as some of Oscar Wilde's. Storytelling for these children should only be undertaken with permission and expert advice; it is wise to talk through the proposed programme with people who know the group well. I have sometimes had severely disturbed children in my audience (without realizing it) and have been told that they listened with absorption, but it was simply my good fortune that the story I had chosen did not distress them in any way.

In the last ten years much has been learned about how children with both mental and physical disablement – particularly the deaf – enjoy and respond to books and stories. The decade has also seen more and more children with special needs being educated in mainstream schools. The National Library for the Handicapped Child, based at the University of London's Institute of Education, provides excellent, experienced advice on telling stories to children with disabilities, who – with forethought on the part of the storyteller – can happily join the audience and sometimes surprise the teller with their mature and articulate understanding of the story.

BOOKS & STORIES MENTIONED

Joan Aiken, 'Humblepuppy', in *A Harp of Fishbones*, Cape

Hans C. Andersen, 'The Emperor's New Clothes' and 'The Ugly Duckling', in Erik Haugaard's *Hans Andersen – His Classic Fairy Tales*, Gollancz, and in *The Faber Book of Favourite Fairy Tales* ed. Sara & Stephen Corrin, Faber

Hans C. Andersen, 'The Snow Queen', in Erik Haugaard's *Hans Andersen – His Classic Fairy Tales*, Gollancz, and in Naomi Lewis's *The Snow Queen*, Walker

Elizabeth Clark, 'Brother Johannick and his Silver Bell', in *The Puffin Book of Christmas Stories* ed. Sara & Stephen Corrin, Puffin

Eileen Colwell, *A Hallowe'en Acorn*, Bodley Head, o.p.

Sara & Stephen Corrin, *The Puffin Book of Christmas Stories*, Puffin

Charles Dickens, 'The Signalman', in Charles Keeping's *Book of Classic Ghost Stories*, Blackie

'hist whist', titled 'Chanson Innocente II', by e.e. cummings, in *Poems for 9 Year-Olds and Under*, ed. Kit Wright, Kestrel / Puffin

Barbara Ireson, *Shadows and Spells*, Faber, o.p.

Ruth Manning-Sanders, *A Book of Ghosts and Goblins*, Methuen, o.p.

Ruth Manning-Sanders, *A Book of Witches, . . . Sorcerers & Spells*, Methuen, o.p.

Philippa Pearce, *The Shadow-Cage*, Puffin

James Reeves, *The Christmas Book*, Heinemann

Ruth Sawyer, 'Schnitzle, Schnotzle and Schnootzle', in *Round the Christmas Tree* ed. Sara & Stephen Corrin, Puffin

'The Water Ghost of Barrowby Hall' by J. K. Bangs, in *Spooks and Spectres* ed. Charles Molin, Puffin, o.p.

Ursula Moray Williams, 'The Good Little Christmas Tree', in *Tell Me Another Story* ed. Eileen Colwell, Young Puffin, and separately in an edition illustrated by Gillian Tyler, Julia MacRae

Additional suggestions

Ghost stories: Alvin Schwartz's *In a Dark Dark Room and Other Scary Stories* (Heinemann, I Can Read); Dinah Starkey's *Ghosts and Bogles* (Heinemann / Pan); Robert Fisher, *Ghosts Galore: Haunting Verse* (Faber)

A Christmas story that could become a tradition: Leon Garfield's *Fair's Fair* (Simon & Schuster)

10

Storytelling
Here and There

In the greater part of this book I have been discussing 'straight' storytelling, that is, telling a story with no props other than the voice and personality of the teller. Various aids, however, can be used to supplement a story, depending on the circumstances and the teller.

In schools storytelling is an important part of children's introduction to books and literature. Storytelling happens most in the infant school, although the idea that only the youngest children enjoy listening to a well-told tale is now acknowledged to be a fallacy, and exciting work is going on in junior and secondary school classrooms. Sadly, even with infants, many teachers read stories rather than telling them. I believe that, during their training, all teachers should receive some tuition and encouragement in storytelling. Often it is only lack of opportunity to learn and observe that inhibits a teacher from storytelling. The new video produced by the Youth Libraries Group is an effective way to provide this opportunity, and should be part of local authority and other in-service days on language and literature.

I have come across various ingenious schemes in schools devised for introducing books and stories. In one I saw teachers and children acting out fairy tales 'in the round', using narration, song and dance. The dialogue was largely impromptu, costume was only suggested, but the story grew before our eyes, a communal effort, joyous and memorable. Another story, 'The Bear Who Wanted to Be a Bird', was set to music by a teacher, with guitar accompaniment. The children – the birds of the story – sang a mocking refrain. The project was a hilarious and exciting occasion for a large audience of children from neighbouring schools. The stories had come to life in an unusual yet traditional way.

Deaf children can be asked to act out a story after it has been told. Usually they will embroider it, while staying within the general outline. They are also very good at discussing and acting their own stories. Children with visual impairment can tell wonderfully imaginative stories, particularly if given a tape recorder.

Most children can become excellent storytellers, but sometimes their lack of experience in expressing themselves in this way causes them to become confused and incoherent. This is tedious for the audience, who are impatient to know what happens next. It is advisable, therefore, to run through the chosen story with the child beforehand so that he or she has more confidence in telling it to other children.

Some children have a flair for storytelling. I remember one girl of ten who told an episode from *Charlotte's Web* with an astonishing wealth of detail and considerable dramatic effect. Why not encourage children to become the storytellers of the future? I once took part in an imaginative project involving one hundred and twenty children in storytelling, poetry and art. The children were inspired to write stories themselves and to illustrate those they had heard. Later they told the stories they especially liked to their schoolmates. It was a happy and stimulating experience for everyone concerned.

Puppets – stringed, glove or finger – can be used effectively in presenting a story, especially to young children. The disadvantage of stringed puppets – marionettes – is that they are complicated to make and require some skill to manipulate, besides needing a curtained-off space behind which the operators can work and a special kind of stage. However, produced as a co-operative effort between teachers or librarians, parents and children, these puppets can present stories in an entrancing and curiously lifelike way. I have found it easy to keep children absorbed in a programme of folk tales and interludes provided by marionettes, but the equipment is cumbersome and the preparation and practice necessarily time-consuming.

Glove puppets are familiar to all children and much simpler to make and use, with or without a portable stage and booth to conceal the operators. They are a development of the ancient Punch and Judy shows, but any traditional story can be used, according to the ingenuity of the puppeteers, frequently the children themselves. I often use a monkey puppet, Jacko, and I find that the fact that the audience *see* me put my hand inside the glove does not detract from the illusion. Children will talk in whispers if I say that Jacko is tired, feed him with 'pretend' bananas (he finds real bananas indigestible) and, after a story, shake hands with him. Because they regard Jacko as a real person, I always tell a story in which he is the chief figure, a combination of my own imagination and some story about a monkey.

Finger puppets, which fit individual fingers like a glove, can represent either people or animals. Finger puppets, one on each hand, can carry on a conversation, for example. Simple nursery tales are suitable material, though the miniature size of finger puppets means they can only be used with small groups.

Both these types of puppets involve children actively, either as operators or as a vociferous audience. A puppeteer usually invites the audience to warn her when the villain of the piece is approaching, a request always obeyed enthusiastically.

Television has come to be regarded as a major source of stories for children, and indeed both *Playschool* and *Jackanory* and similar subsequent programmes have been the means of introducing a wide selection of stories to young audiences. I was one of the first storytellers on *Playschool* when the programme began in 1964. In those days I was left free to tell a simple story of my own choice without the aid of pictures. With the advent of colour television, it became possible to present picture books in a variety of attractive and imaginative ways to young children.

Jackanory, in which I was also involved in the early days, used a different method of telling stories from any I have mentioned. When I gave a programme of Eleanor Farjeon's stories on *Jackanory* I found that I could not tell the stories as I would in the library but was required to read from a prepared script into which music and film had been interpolated. Today, a whole book rather than a single story is read in planned instalments by professional actors or actresses and illustrated by film. Alternatively, a book becomes a film in its own right as, for example, John Masefield's *A Box of Delights* and Philippa Pearce's *Tom's Midnight Garden*.

All these programmes suffer – from the storyteller's point of view – from having to be presented to technicians and producers rather than to an audience of children. It is claimed that the combination of vision and sound has brought back the oral tradition, but the direct and *live* relationship between story and child, in which I so strongly believe, is crucially missing.

Stories are also told on video cassettes and film strips in which voice, pictures and perhaps music are all part of the story. In my opinion the best selection is still produced by Weston Woods, a firm specializing in the reproduction of such children's favourites as *Peter Rabbit*, *The Snowman*, *Morris's Disappearing Bag* among many others. I have seen a group of young children watch the animated film of Pat Hutchins's *Rosie's Walk*, accompanied by the catchy tune of 'Turkey in the Straw', three times over and still demand another showing. This kind of storytelling adds variety when a live storyteller is not available. It also opens the door to literature for children who cannot read, for those whose physical disabilities mean they can't handle a printed book, and for deaf children who gain more from the visual presentation than they might from a told story.

There is now a vast range of audio-visual material, and for children who cannot use print in any form, it is invaluable; Caedmon, Cover to Cover (Puffin) and Cornerstone are among the firms now producing well-chosen children's stories on tape. Story recordings are of doubtful value with groups of children, there being no focal point to hold their attention. The absence of a personal relationship is a drawback, for the faceless storyteller cannot adjust to the audience. However, an individual child can enjoy listening by himself, for this means that the story becomes a personal exchange between unseen storyteller and child.

Video cassettes, films, tapes, are all a somewhat artificial way of telling stories and can never be an adequate substitute for live storytelling. This is still to be found in many parts of the world. In countries where there are fewer forms of entertainment, traditional storytelling has more chance of survival, although today it is threatened by the all-powerful and ubiquitous use of television. Among the nomadic desert peoples, in the tropical islands of the South Seas, in the colourful markets of Africa and the bazaars of India, storytellers still pass on their native folk tales to the next generation by word of mouth. The spider man of the West Indies, the trolls and giants of Scandinavia, the djinns of Arabia, the fairy folk of Britain, the Baba Yagas of Russia are known to boys and girls of the twentieth century as they were to children hundreds of years ago.

When I first told stories in libraries and elsewhere in the 1920s, I had few companions in the art. Over the years storytelling found its place in libraries but little interest was shown in the community. Today storytelling is no longer confined to schools and libraries, and although most libraries still have a picture-book storytime for younger children, and stories for older children during book weeks, storytelling has become a wider, community activity. In Britain the influence of Rani Singh, Duncan Williamson, and Grace Hallworth is particularly notable.

In the last decade or so, the art of storytelling has spread not only in Britain but in other countries. There is a Storytellers' School in Canada, and in Japan the Tokyo Children's Library organizes courses in storytelling for the mothers in the neighbourhood. In Australia, where Story has always been a significant influence in the traditional life of the Aboriginal peoples, storytelling is having a modern revival in all the Australian states, under the inspiration of the Storytellers' Guild. In the United States there has been an interest in storytelling for years, and many associations and individual storytellers now foster the art in the community; in New York's Central Park there is regular storytelling every summer. In the United Kingdom we now have a College of Storytellers and a Company of Storytellers amongst a number of such associations. The National Folktale Society has listed nearly one hundred professional storytellers, among whom is a traveller with three thousand tales in his repertoire. The first Birmingham Storytelling Festival was held in the summer of 1990, celebrating stories from every continent. Everywhere there seems to be a spontaneous desire for the preservation and active sharing of the oral tradition.

Storytelling associations and societies hold annual workshops and festivals where stories are told in many exciting ways, sometimes in costume, to the accompaniment of music or dance or puppets. Such festivals can be inspiring occasions. I remember a storytelling festival that was part of an American Library Association Conference, held at Miami Beach. Storytellers from Japan, Germany, the West Indies, Ireland, the Southern States of America, and Britain told stories to a large audience of librarians (and *one* child) in the incongruous setting of a nightclub. Another notable festival was held at Boys and Girls House, Toronto, a library in which there has always been storytelling since Lillian Smith, the eminent librarian, established the tradition in the first half of the century. On this occasion the programme included the three ways of telling stories – in speech, song and dance. Indian children in tribal dress presented a traditional story in dance and mime, a singer sang sea shanties that embodied a narrative; experienced storytellers told folk tales from various cultures. The Third International Storytelling Festival in London (1989) brought together forty-one storytellers from ten countries, with events in many parts of the country as well. It is notable that such festivals attract both adults and children.

An additional indication of the growing importance of storytelling in the modern world is the interest shown by television. A four-part programme about various aspects of storytelling was screened in the U.K. early in 1990. It included storytellers from varied backgrounds and nationalities telling stories directly to a live audience in a variety of environments.

All these storytelling activities concern the revival and dissemination of stories to all age groups. In the main, traditional material is used, which helps to keep alive the ethnic folk literature so important for the shifting populations of the world today. The exchange of stories helps communication not only between cultures but between generations. Storytelling is a force in the modern world as it was in the ancient world.

I can do no better than conclude with a poet and storyteller's hope for storytelling. John Masefield was himself a wonderful storyteller whose experience of telling stories to hundreds of audiences had convinced him that men and women enjoy stories and can be deeply moved by them. In 1961 I was privileged, as 'Guest Storyteller' and Masefield's personal friend, to convey his recorded message to the Storytelling Festival in his honour at Toronto. In it he said:

> I hope that, in time, little groups of storytellers will be telling the great tales of the world to the multitudes now and always longing to hear them told newly, told memorably, told again.

Surely this is the desire of all who love stories.

BOOKS & STORIES MENTIONED

'The Bear Who Wanted to Be a Bird', by A. & C. de Leeuw, in *Tell Me a Story*, ed. Eileen Colwell, Young Puffin
E.B. White, *Charlotte's Web*, Hamish Hamilton / Puffin
Weston Woods, 14 Friday Street, Henley-on-Thames, Oxfordshire RG9 1AH

100 + STORYTELLING SOURCES

This listing, compiled from recommendations made by Beverley Mathias and Mary Steele, complements and extends the end-of-chapter booklists. Mary Steele comments: 'No such listing can be comprehensive; the following titles have been selected on the basis of "You won't go far wrong if you try these". Readers may extend the range of their searching by looking out for other books by the writers and illustrators listed below and at the end of chapters.'

COLLECTIONS COMPILED BY EILEEN COLWELL

In print:
Bad Boys, Young Puffin
Bedtime Stories, Ladybird
High Days and Holidays, Viking Kestrel / Young Puffin
More Stories to Tell, Young Puffin
Tell Me a Story, Young Puffin
Tell Me Another Story, Young Puffin
Time for a Story, Young Puffin

(Out of print but likely to be available in libraries: *Humblepuppy*; *The Magic Umbrella*; *A Storyteller's Choice*; *A Second Storyteller's Choice*; *The Youngest Storybook* [all Bodley Head]; *Roundabout and Long Ago* [Longman Young Books]; *Tales from the Islands* [Kestrel])

PICTURE BOOKS

Janet & Allan Ahlberg, *Each Peach Pear Plum*, Viking Kestrel / Picture Puffin
Janet & Allan Ahlberg, *Peepo!*, Viking Kestrel / Picture Puffin
Janet & Allan Ahlberg, *Bye Bye Baby*, Heinemann
Pamela Allen, *Who Sank the Boat?*, Hamish Hamilton / Picture Puffin
Ronda & David Armitage, *The Lighthouse Keeper's Lunch*, Deutsch / Picture Puffin
Quentin Blake, *Mr Magnolia*, Cape / Picture Puffin
Ruth Brown, *Our Cat Flossie*, Andersen / Beaver

Anthony Browne, *Gorilla*, Julia MacRae / Mammoth
Anthony Browne, *Willy the Champ*, Julia MacRae / Mammoth
Rod Campbell, *Dear Zoo*, Campbell Blackie / Picture Puffin
Lynley Dodd, *Hairy McClary from Donaldson's Dairy*, Spindlewood / Picture Puffin
Mairi Hedderwick, *Katie Morag Delivers the Mail*, Bodley Head / Picture Lion
Shirley Hughes, *Alfie Gets in First*, Bodley Head / Picture Lion
Shirley Hughes, *Dogger*, Bodley Head / Picture Lion
Jack Kent, *The Fat Cat*, Picture Puffin
Jack Kent, *There's No Such Thing as a Dragon*, Blackie
Judith Kerr, *Mog the Forgetful Cat*, Collins, hardback and paperback
David McPhail, *Where Can an Elephant Hide?*, Deutsch / Magnet
Jill Murphy, *Peace at Last*, Macmillan / Picturemac
Jill Murphy, *Whatever Next!*, Macmillan / Picturemac
Mary Rees, *Ten in a Bed*, Andersen / Little Mammoth
Gerald Rose, *The Bag of Wind*, Bodley Head / Magnet
Michael Rosen & Helen Oxenbury, *We're Going on a Bear Hunt*, Walker
Kathy Stinson, *Red is Best*, Oxford University Press, hardback and paperback
Eve Sutton & Lynley Dodd, *My Cat Likes to Hide in Boxes*, Spindlewood / Picture Puffin
Jenny Wagner & Ron Brooks, *John Brown, Rose and the Midnight Cat*, Viking Kestrel / Puffin
Rosemary Wells, *Noisy Nora*, Collins / Picture Lion

STORYTIME COLLECTIONS

(△ indicates much-used basic titles that are also referenced in the booklists at the end of each chapter.)
Joan Aiken, *Necklace of Raindrops*, Cape / Puffin
Joan Aiken, *Tale of a One-Way Street*, Cape / Puffin
△ *Hans Andersen: His Classic Fairy Tales*, translated by Erik Haugaard, Gollancz
Floella Benjamin, *Why the Agouti Has No Tail*, Hutchinson
Leila Berg, *Tales for Telling*, Methuen / Magnet
Ann Cameron, *The Julian Stories*, Gollancz / Lions
Laura Cecil, *Listen to This*, Bodley Head / Red Fox
Laura Cecil, *Stuff and Nonsense*, Bodley Head
Sara & Stephen Corrin, *The Puffin Book of Modern Fairy Tales*, Puffin, 8 up

△ Sara & Stephen Corrin, *More Stories for Under-Fives*, Faber / Young Puffin
The Corrins have compiled many thematic and age-related collections of stories that are widely used and recommended.
Kevin Crossley-Holland, *Folk Tales of the British Isles*, Faber, 8 up
△ Judith Elkin, *The New Golden Land Anthology*, Viking Kestrel / Puffin
Clifton Fadiman, *The Puffin Treasury of Favourite Stories*, Viking Kestrel / Puffin
△ Alan Garner, *Book of British Fairy Tales*, Collins, 8 up
Jamila Gavin, *Three Indian Princesses*, Methuen, 8 up
Iris Grender, *Did I Ever Tell You . . .* stories, Hutchinson
△ *The Brothers Grimm: Popular Folk Tales*, trans. Brian Alderson, Gollancz
Grace Hallworth, *Listen to This Story*, Methuen / Magnet
Grace Hallworth, *Mouth Open, Story Jump Out*, Methuen / Magnet, 8 up
Grace Hallworth, *Cric Crac*, Heinemann
Grace Hallworth, *A Web of Stories*, Methuen
David L. Harrison, *A Book of Giant Stories*, Cape
△ Virginia Haviland, *The Fairy Tale Treasury*, Hamish Hamilton / Picture Puffin
Kathleen Hersom, *Johnny Reed's Cat and Other Northern Tales*, Black
Ted Hughes, *How the Whale Became*, Young Puffin
△ Joseph Jacobs, *English Fairy Tales*, Dover; a selection in Puffin
△ Julius Lester, *The Tales of Uncle Remus: The Adventures of Brer Rabbit*, Bodley Head / Pan
Naomi Lewis, *Stories from the Arabian Nights*, Methuen, 8 up
△ Kathleen Lines, *The Faber Storybook*, Faber
Margaret Mahy, *Leaf Magic and Five Other Favourites*, Dent / Magnet
Margaret Mahy, *Mahy Magic*, Dent
Jan Mark, *Nothing to Be Afraid Of*, Viking / Puffin, 8 up
△ Pamela Oldfield, *Stories from Ancient Greece*, Kingfisher
Philippa Pearce, *What the Neighbours Did*, Puffin, 8 up
△ Charles Perrault, *Sleeping Beauty and Other Favourite Fairy Tales*, translated by Angela Carter, Gollancz
Saviour Pirotta, *Storyworld*, Blackie
Chris Powling, *Fingers Crossed*, Blackie / Knight
Susan Price, *The Kingfisher Treasury of Nursery Stories*, Kingfisher
William Radice, *The Stupid Tiger*, Deutsch, 8 up
△ Anne Rockwell, *The Story of the Three Bears and 15 Other Stories*, Hamish Hamilton / Puffin

Michael Rosen, *Funny Stories*, Kingfisher, 8 up
Michael Rosen, *The Wicked Tricks of Till Owlyglass*, Walker, 8 up
Rani Singh, *The Indian Storybook*, Heinemann, hardback and paperback
Fiona Waters, *The Cat King's Daughter*, Magnet
Amabel Williams-Ellis, *The Enchanted World*, Hodder / Premier Picturemac (2 vols.)

POETRY

John Agard, *I Din Do Nuttin*, Magnet
John Agard, *Say it Again, Granny*, Magnet
Allan Ahlberg, *Please Mrs Butler*, Viking Kestrel / Puffin
Allan Ahlberg, *Heard It in the Playground*, Viking Kestrel / Puffin
Jill Bennett, *Roger Was a Razor Fish*, Bodley Head / Hippo
Jill Bennett, *Singing in the Sun*, Young Puffin
Edward Blishen, *The Oxford Book of Poetry for Children*, Oxford University Press
Marc Brown, *Hand Rhymes*, Collins / Picture Lion
Charles Causley, *Jack the Treacle Eater*, Macmillan / Picturemac
Wendy Cope, *Twiddling Your Thumbs: Hand Rhymes*, Faber
John Foster, *Let's Celebrate: Festival Poems*, Oxford University Press
Anne Harvey, *Of Caterpillars, Cats and Cattle*, Viking Kestrel / Puffin
Ted Hughes & Seamus Heaney, compilers, *The Rattle Bag*, Faber
Beverley Mathias, *Shout, Whisper & Sing*, Bodley Head
Mother Goose, illustrated by Tomie dePaola, Methuen
Mother Goose Treasury, illustrated by Raymond Briggs, Hamish Hamilton / Picture Puffin
Grace Nichols, *Come on into My Tropical Garden*, Black
Judith Nicholls, *Midnight Forest*, Faber, 8 up
Michael Rosen, *Quick, Let's Get Out of Here*, Deutsch / Puffin
Michael Rosen, *The Kingfisher Book of Children's Poetry*, Kingfisher
Morag Styles, *I Like This Stuff*, Cambridge University Press
Sarah Williams, *Round and Round the Garden*, Oxford University Press, hardback and paperback
Raymond Wilson, *Every Poem Tells a Story*, Puffin
Kit Wright, *Poems for 9 Year-Olds and Under*, Puffin

ABOUT STORYTELLING

By Word of Mouth, publication accompanying Channel 4 television programme, Channel 4, P.O. Box 4000, London W3 6XJ

Betty Rosen, *And None of it Was Nonsense: The Power of Storytelling in School*, Mary Glasgow Publications, Avenue House, 131-133 Holland Park Avenue, London W11 4UT

Liz Weir, editor, *Telling the Tale: A Storytelling Guide*, Youth Libraries Group (Remploy; see address below)

Video by Grace Hallworth & Liz Weir, *Tell Me Another One! Storytelling Through Picture Books*, Youth Libraries Group (Remploy Ltd, London Road, Newcastle-under-Lyme, Staffordshire)

A Directory of Storytellers, compiled by Linda Cotterill and Helen East, has been produced by the National Folktale and Storytelling Centre and is available from Children's Book Foundation, Book House, 45 East Hill, London SW18 2QZ.

Address for The College of Storytellers: Freepost, London NW3 4YB.
Address for the Company of Storytellers: c/o The Studio, 27 St Peter's Square, Hammersmith, London W6 9NW.

The development of multicultural education has been a significant factor in the revival of interest in storytelling in recent years. Comprehensive advice may be found in *The Books for Keeps Guide to Children's Books for a Multicultural Society*, presently (autumn 1990) being revised by Judith Elkin; details from *Books for Keeps*, 6 Brightfield Road, Lee, London SE12 8QF.